DIESELS DIVERTED

DIESELS DIVERTED

40 YEARS OF DIVERTED TRAINS 1980–2020

KIM FULLBROOK

First published in Great Britain in 2022 by
Pen and Sword Transport
An imprint of
Pen & Sword Books Ltd.
Yorkshire - Philadelphia

Copyright © Kim Fullbrook, 2022

ISBN 978 1 39909 476 4

The right of Kim Fullbrook to be identified as author of this work has been asserted by him in accordance with the Copyright, Designs and Patents Act 1988.

A CIP catalogue record for this book is available from the British Library.

All rights reserved. No part of this book may be reproduced or transmitted in any form or by any means, electronic or mechanical including photocopying, recording or by any information storage and retrieval system, without permission from the Publisher in writing.

Typeset in 11/13.5 pt Times New Roman
by SJmagic DESIGN SERVICES, India.
Printed and bound in India by Replika Press Pvt. Ltd.

Pen & Sword Books Ltd incorporates the imprints of Pen & Sword Books Archaeology, Atlas, Aviation, Battleground, Discovery, Family History, History, Maritime, Military, Naval, Politics, Railways, Select, Transport, True Crime, Fiction, Frontline Books, Leo Cooper, Praetorian Press, Seaforth Publishing, Wharncliffe and White Owl.

For a complete list of Pen & Sword titles please contact

PEN & SWORD BOOKS LIMITED
47 Church Street, Barnsley, South Yorkshire, S70 2AS, England
E-mail: enquiries@pen-and-sword.co.uk
Website: www.pen-and-sword.co.uk

or

PEN AND SWORD BOOKS
1950 Lawrence Rd, Havertown, PA 19083, USA
E-mail: Uspen-and-sword@casematepublishers.com
Website: www.penandswordbooks.com

Introduction

When preparing this book I searched through my photographic collection for pictures showing diverted trains and found a broad selection covering the last forty years. Nevertheless, there were a few notable diversions or locations that weren't covered and I'm very grateful to those photographers who have kindly supplied pictures from their collections to fill these gaps. I cannot claim that every diversion is represented or that there is even coverage across the country but most areas are represented and there is plenty of variety. East and West Coast main line diversions predominate as these are the UK's most important main lines. Some of the diversions shown here are very obscure and some feature lines that are now closed so, when reading this book, it will help to have current and historic rail atlases to hand. There are several instances of pictures taken years apart at the same location which illustrate the amount of change. Generally, pictures appear in chronological order although there is a handful of exceptions where pictures taken in a particular area at around the same time have been grouped. The title of the book is Diesels Diverted as the majority of workings are worked by diesel locomotives and units, but a small number of electrics also appear. All photos have been taken by me, except where credited to other photographers.

Why the interest in Diversions ?

I first dabbled in photography after receiving a Zenit E camera as a Christmas present in 1976. Occasionally, I travelled my local area by train and took fairly poor photos of what I saw. The Zenit was very restricting, and I bought a Chinon CE II with the aim of making the process of taking pictures easier. It was only after becoming a student and joining the Cambridge University Railway Club that my interest in photography fully developed as I went on trips with other club members. At a club meeting in April 1980, another member told us that East Coast Main Line services were due to be diverted via Cambridge early on Sunday mornings for the next two weeks. This gave the prospect of seeing Deltics on workings that would not normally pass through Cambridge and sounded quite interesting. The thought of a really early start on a Sunday morning was not attractive but the novelty of photographing a Deltic locally had some appeal, so I resolved to make the effort. The first Sunday had quite dull weather and although I managed some shots my technique was not particularly good. The second Sunday was sunny and I got some better results. Compared to what was normally on offer at Cambridge, capturing these unusual workings gave a feeling of achievement. Some of these pictures are included at the beginning of the book. Later in the year, I replaced the Chinon with a much better camera – a Canon AE1 – and as I went on trips with other photographers my results began to improve.

On 1 February 1982, I heard on the radio news that there had been an earth slip on the East Coast Main Line near Grantham and trains were being diverted. This meant trains leaving the main line at Peterborough for Spalding and going via the GN & GE joint line to Doncaster. This was of particular interest because the GN & GE joint was one of my favourite lines and normally saw few trains. With the diversions there was the prospect of getting a good number of shots along the line. As the weather forecast for 2 February was sunny and my academic workload for the next day could be re-arranged, I went by train with a friend to Spalding, taking our bikes so that we could cycle to Sleaford via numerous railway crossings and overbridges.

These early experiences set the scene for the future. Diversions offered the chance to see regular timetabled trains running on different lines. Often this meant a much-increased frequency of service compared to a normal day and there might be loco-hauled trains where there would usually only be units. On some lines you could see electric trains being hauled by diesel locomotives – termed a 'drag' by enthusiasts. Most diversions were at weekends which allowed me to get out more easily to see them as I worked on weekdays. The most sought-after diversions involved passenger trains running on freight only lines and freight trains being diverted over unusual routes. In the mid-1980s I lived in Manchester and managed to track down a variety of diversions throughout the area. Unfortunately, the combination of slow colour slide films and frequently cloudy weather in the area meant that I took most of these pictures only on black & white negative film and they do not appear here.

Use of Diversionary Routes

British Rail had a policy of diverting trains around engineering work where feasible and a wide range of diversions could be found through to the early 1990s. The major diversions using the Settle & Carlisle and Nuneaton routes got plenty of attention from enthusiasts with photographs appearing in the railway magazines, but the smaller and more obscure diversions got little publicity. While researching this book, I found out about numerous local diversions which I had not been aware of previously. Rail privatisation from 1996 restructured and fragmented the industry, cutting the number of diversions. For a time, the privatised companies GNER and Virgin Trains rediscovered the advantages to passengers of maintaining rail services and from 1997 onwards it seemed that there would be a major set of diversions every bank holiday weekend.

Sadly, since the early 2000s new train companies have taken over most lines and usually preferred to organise buses to run around a blocked line rather than run trains over diversionary routes. This has been unpopular with passengers and the term 'rail replacement bus' became a joke in the media. When diversions have been organised, they tend to be small, localised affairs.

Information

In the 1980s and '90s, information on diversions could be hard to find. The Passenger Timetable usually had times for diversions that lasted several weeks but shorter arrangements did not appear. The railway's own Weekly Operating Notice was the ideal source, but you had to know someone who had access to it. Enthusiast magazines sometimes had information as did the Branch Line Society's newsletter. In the 1990s and 2000s a very good source for nationwide information was the now-defunct Teletext which had a page on BBC2 devoted to forthcoming service changes. I spent many hours watching these pages refreshing and trying to figure out if there would be diversions or not. Now, in the Internet Age, we have enthusiast websites full of information as well as specialist web sites providing access to copies of train schedules and the track diagrams used in the network control centres. It seems that as the ease of finding out what is happening has improved the number of opportunities has declined.

Locomotives

Up to the 1990s, HSTs and the ubiquitous class 47 diesels were the most common motive power for diversions. With British Rail the class 47s were very much the universal locomotive and featured on many passenger and freight trains. Until the mid-1980s Class 37, 40, 45 and 55 diesels appeared too on some lines. Freight engines like Classes 56 and 58 appeared occasionally in the 1980s and early 1990s but I never succeeded in capturing them on film. As Class 47s disappeared from front line use, Classes 57 and 67 were used.

West Coast diversions operated by Virgin Trains feature throughout this book, particularly via Nuneaton as these were common in the period 1997-2006 and it is interesting to see how the Class 47 sub-classes and liveries have varied during that time. RES (Rail Express Systems), EWS red, Railfreight grey and Virgin Cross Country have all appeared regularly plus a few oddments on isolated occasions. When Pendolino units were introduced to replace the Mark 2 and 3 coaches, Class 57s (themselves converted from Class 47s) in Virgin livery were used when these units had to be hauled. With the West Coast Upgrade project complete, there have been fewer diversions and more rail replacement bus services. On the East Coast route, a variety of Class 47s were hired by GNER to drag electric locomotive hauled sets, then EWS Class 67s took over after the 47s were withdrawn.

Acknowledgements

I would like to thank the following people who helped me both directly and indirectly with the creation of this book. Ian Capper, Michael Rhodes and Paul Shannon provided much assistance as my interest in photography developed during 1980. Steve Barrow, Gordon Bird, Paul Davis and Rod Nelson provided support on trips to photograph diversions. Shaun Courtnage created an archive on his Class 47 List web site which helped me check some captions. John Cowburn reviewed an early draft of the book. Brian Carter, Paul

Davis, Stewart Jolly, Les Nixon and John Turner supplied photographs. Special thanks are due to Antony Guppy for his help in several areas: providing information on numerous diversions over the years, supplying photographs and reviewing an early draft of the book. Last and not least, my wife Petra provided much encouragement and support.

Kim Fullbrook
Maidenhead,
October 2022

Rear Cover Upper HST
The East Coast Main Line through Grantham has been closed at short notice due to an earth slip and trains are being diverted over the Great Northern & Great Eastern Joint Line through Spalding. A northbound HST from King's Cross passes through Gosberton. 2 February 1982

Rear Cover Middle Virgin 57
Diversions via Nuneaton were much less common once the upgrades on the main West Coast route had been completed in the early 2000s. Nevertheless, on the weekend of 15/16 July 2006 diverted services were operated with Class 390 Pendolino units hauled by Class 57s. In full Virgin Trains livery, 57309 tows Pendolino 390020 around the sharp curve from Nuneaton station towards Abbey Junction while working the 13.20 Euston-Wolverhampton. 15 July 2006

Rear Cover Lower 66539
The North London line through Highbury & Islington has been closed for rebuilding work and through freight trains are being diverted via the non-electrified Gospel Oak-Barking line. Those Freightliner trains that are normally electrically hauled have a Class 66 added to the front to provide diesel haulage. 66539 + 90044 approach South Tottenham station working a Crewe-Felixstowe container train. 29 May 2009

Front Cover Top
Trains between Wolverhampton and Euston are being diverted via Water Orton and Nuneaton while the Birmingham-Rugby line through Coventry is closed for engineering work. Fragonset's 47703 tows 87032 on the 16.15 Euston-Wolverhampton and is seen in open countryside near Daw Mill. 18 July 1998

Front Cover Main
On August Bank Holiday Sunday in 2000 the East Coast main line was closed between Newark and Doncaster with trains being diverted via Gainsborough and Lincoln. 47734 rounds the curve north of Saxilby with the 10.00 Edinburgh Waverley-King's Cross. 91010 is out of sight on the rear. 27 August 2000

Inside flap
On Easter Saturday and Sunday in 1998 the East Coast main line was closed between Darlington and Newcastle so trains were diverted via the Durham Coast line. With a storm over the sea in the background, 47772 towing 91030 on the 12.45 Glasgow Central-King's Cross leaves Seaham. 12 April 1998

List of Abbreviations

DRS	Direct Rail Services. A freight train operating company
DVT	Driving Van Trailer. A driving cab on an unpowered coach normally used to control a locomotive at the other end of the train
EWS	English, Welsh and Scottish Railways, a rail freight company since 1995, taken over by Deutsche Bahn and rebranded as DB Cargo
GBRF	Great Britain Rail Freight, a freight railway company
GN & GE	Great Northern and Great Eastern Railway. A railway line from Huntingdon to Doncaster via March and Lincoln.
GNER	Great North Eastern Railway. A train operating company on the East Coast main line from 1996 to 2007
GWR	Great Western Railway. A passenger train operating company serving Western England and South Wales since 1996
HST	High Speed Train
LNER	London & North Eastern Railway. A train operating company on the East Coast main line since 2018
RES	Rail Express Systems. A sector of British Rail that was responsible for transport of mail and parcels. Later taken over by EWS.

In April 1980, the East Coast main line through Huntingdon was closed before 9am on two Sunday mornings with a handful of overnight trains diverted via Cambridge. This was my first photo of a diverted train and inspired my interest in trains on unusual routes. 55007 passes Cambridge South with the 19.15 Aberdeen-King's Cross. It was the first of two overnight trains from Aberdeen and was formed of just regular seated coaches without any sleeping cars. The new Cambridge power signal box can be seen under construction on the left. 20 April 1980

The second set of diversions took place on Sunday 27 April. I went to the footbridge on Chesterton Common for the first train in daylight hours and was rewarded by the sight of 46049 appearing through the early morning mist with the 19.15 Aberdeen-King's Cross. This was the only time I saw a Class 46 in the Cambridge area. The girder bridge in the background crosses the River Cam. Beyond it can be seen the roof of Chesterton Junction signal box which at the time controlled the junction for the freight-only branch to Fen Drayton. The signal box closed in 1984 and the branch in 1992. Cambridge North station was opened in 2017 just beyond the former junction. 27 April 1980

I cycled quickly to the Mill Road bridge in Cambridge where there was less mist and the sun had appeared. At 8am the second overnight train from Aberdeen arrived: the 20.05 to King's Cross headed by 55017. This train has only Mark 1 sleeper coaches and parcel vans with no coaches for seated passengers. Much rebuilding work had been taking place in preparation for re-signalling in 1982. In the background can be seen Coldhams Lane Signal Box and Depot. 27 April 1980

No apologies for including a second shot of 55017 as there is so much to see in this picture and most of it has disappeared from the railway. A little wisp of steam heating can be seen at the front of the loco. In 1980 sleeper services ran every night of the week but since then the network has been drastically reduced and services have not run on Saturday nights since 1994/5. The stabling point is full of locos, the carriage sidings are well filled with Mark 1 coaches and there is an old steam tender in the far siding. Cambridge North signal box and its semaphores will survive another two years until closure due to re-signalling in 1982. 27 April 1980

On Sunday 4 May 1980 the Glasgow-Edinburgh main line through Falkirk High station was closed for engineering work so trains were diverted. The routing for these workings after leaving Glasgow Queen Street involved reversing at Cowlairs as the south curve was not built until 1992. After reversal, trains took the line through Springburn and the spur to Gartcosh Junction, then Carmuirs Junction and Falkirk Grahamston before regaining their normal route at Polmont. 47709 pushes the 17.00 Glasgow Queen Street-Edinburgh Waverley through Springburn station. 4 May 1980. (Antony Guppy)

A little further on from the previous picture, 47706 propels the 18.00 Glasgow Queen Street-Edinburgh Waverley round the curve between Sighthill Junction and Sighthill East Junction. In the background can be seen the sidings outside St Rollox works. On the left is the electrified suburban line to Springburn station used by services through Glasgow Queen Street Low Level. Class 47s working push pull sets with DBSO driving trailers had been introduced on Glasgow-Edinburgh services the previous year. 4 May 1980. (Antony Guppy)

Due to engineering work on the Hope Valley line on Sundays through much of 1980/1, passenger trains were frequently diverted over the Woodhead route, despite its closure having been announced. On a snowy spring day, the 12.15 Sheffield Midland-Manchester Piccadilly heads west near Thurlestone, formed of a Class 124 Trans Pennine DMU. Just four months later, the main section of the line through the Pennines was closed between Penistone and Hadfield (including the Woodhead Tunnel) less than thirty years after the 1500V DC electrification was completed. 22 March 1981. (Les Nixon)

After an earth slip on the East Coast main line near Grantham on 1 February 1982, a reduced service of trains was diverted via the GN & GE joint line on the next day. The weather at Spalding station was initially dull and misty as a King's Cross-bound HST passes through. At the time, Spalding was one of my favourite locations and later pictures in this book show just how much the area has been rationalised. I was disappointed at the time that the trains were all HSTs and only hourly in each direction. I did not see any diverted freights, just the regular flyash to Fletton. 2 February 1982

A southbound HST for King's Cross passes Gosberton. There are extra staff in the cab providing route knowledge for this diversion. Long disappeared features of this location worth noting are the full set of telegraph wires on the left, the down goods loop and the concrete support post for a wire holding up the semaphore signal. This is my favourite countryside photographic location on the line and a view from 2008 appears on page 94. 2 February 1982

An HST heading for King's Cross is seen across the fields approaching Brewery Lane level crossing, north of Spalding. The flat nature of the land in this area is clear to see. Gosberton water tower – a local landmark at the time but no longer standing – is visible behind the train. The railway house beside the level crossing has since been demolished and the crossing gates replaced by remotely controlled barriers. 2 February 1982

In the 1983 summer timetable, the Midland Main Line between Leicester and Kettering was planned to be closed up to 1600 on Sundays. 45150 + 108 are in charge of the 13.05 Nottingham-St Pancras as it passes Glendon Sidings, near Kettering. This was one of the few loco hauled trains left after HSTs had taken over most of the services and was commonly double headed as a positioning move. The line in the right foreground once led to extensive sidings serving the nearby ironstone quarries. Since 1994 the site has been redeveloped to become the Barford Meadow Nature Reserve. Glendon Sidings signal box was switched out at the time of this photograph – a common sign of impending closure – and was closed just a few months later in November 1983. 3 July 1983

When these diversions were in operation, trains from the north heading to St Pancras ran into Leicester, then reversed and travelled back to Syston Junction where they turned east and ran via Melton Mowbray and Corby to reach London. An HST set forming the 12.40 Derby-St Pancras is seen at Glendon South Junction, north of Kettering, a short distance further on from the picture above. 3 July 1983

In east London there are only a few places where diversionary routes exist, one being the Lea Valley. The Lea Valley main line through Tottenham Hale was closed all weekend on 13/14 August 1983 due to work in Clapton Tunnel with Liverpool Street to Cambridge and Kings Lynn trains being diverted via the line through Seven Sisters known as the Southbury Loop. 37110 approaches Theobalds Grove with the 11.35 Liverpool St-Cambridge. 13 August 1983

From 13 November 1983 to the end of the 1983/4 timetable on 13 May 1984, Sunday morning trains from Glasgow were diverted via the Glasgow & South Western and Settle & Carlisle lines. To reach the West Coast main line at Preston these trains took the Hellifield-Blackburn line where we see 47403 hauling the 09.20 Glasgow-Paddington across the impressive 48-arch brick viaduct at Whalley, known as Whalley Arches. 15 April 1984

In the Manchester area there were diversions most Sundays. On 1 July 1984 Trans Pennine services to Liverpool ran via Guide Bridge, Piccadilly, Glazebrook and Warrington Central instead of Victoria, Eccles and St Helens Junction. 47588 crosses the high bridge over the Manchester Ship Canal at Irlam with the 11.55 Newcastle-Liverpool Lime Street. The Glazebrook line had no timetabled loco hauled passenger trains at the time, but this changed in the 1989/90 timetable when Trans Pennine services were re-routed over the line instead of calling at Manchester Victoria. The land in the foreground was the site of Irlam steelworks which finally closed in 1979. It is now the site of a large industrial estate and the main A57 road has been diverted to run under the bridge along the route of the former Manchester Ship Canal railway. 1 July 1984

Engineering work on the Rugby-Coventry-Birmingham line was common on Sundays in the 1980s, with trains being diverted via Nuneaton. As this line was not electrified, diesel haulage was required, although the electric locomotive was kept in the formation so it could be used on the Birmingham-Wolverhampton part of the journey. The ubiquitous Class 47 was most commonly used but Class 58 freight locomotives were often employed after their introduction in 1983. 58014 and 86239 pass Abbey Junction at Nuneaton working the 12.00 Euston-Wolverhampton. 1 July 1984. (John Turner)

The stone trains between Northwich and Tunstead were booked to run every day including Sundays, which meant diversions could happen when weekend engineering work took place. Normally these trains ran via Skelton Junction (Altrincham) and Northenden Junction to New Mills South Junction but eastbound trains between Northenden Junction and New Mills South Junction had stopped running from 29 April 1984 when Cheadle Junction signal box was severely damaged in an arson attack. Working in both directions was restored from 15 July 1984 and the line was singled. 20186 + 077 have been diverted via Manchester Oxford Road where they are seen with Northwich-Tunstead stone empties. The route taken was via Sale, Oxford Road and Ashburys, then either via Guide Bridge and Hyde North to Romiley or direct via Reddish North to Romiley, picking up the normal route at New Mills South Junction. 8 July 1984

In the 1984/5 timetable, West Coast main line services were diverted through Manchester on Saturday nights and part of Sunday from the start of the timetable in mid-May through to the end of October. The routing was initially via Piccadilly and the Castlefield route to/from Stockport, then changed to Victoria and the Ashton Moss route on 2 September. Here we see 47437 + 86315 on the 09.45 Euston to Glasgow Central between Manchester Piccadilly and Oxford Road stations. It will shortly turn right at Castlefield Junction to Ordsall Lane Junction and take the line through Eccles towards Parkside Junction where it will re-join the West Coast Main Line. At the time, these were the only booked passenger trains to use the section of line between Castlefield Junction and Ordsall Lane Junction. 8 July 1984

47413 + 86326 pass Ordsall Lane Junction, Manchester, with the 09.45 Euston- Glasgow. At this time the Windsor link to the Bolton line had not yet been built so the train could only take the Eccles route to reach Preston via Parkside Junction. The sidings in the foreground served Ordsall Lane freight terminal and were also used for reversal by a daily parcels working between Victoria, Piccadilly and Mayfield which was operated by a Class 128 diesel parcels unit. The view of the Manchester skyline has changed radically since 1984 with many new apartment blocks built. 19 August 1984

Class 37s were rarely seen on Nuneaton diversions, but a pair appeared on 8 July 1984. 37206 + 37176 + 86252 pass Bromford Bridge on the outskirts of Birmingham with the 12.00 Euston-Wolverhampton. The sidings on the left full of yellow internal user wagons loaded with pipes belong to the British Steel Corporation Bromford plant. In the far left background are the sidings of the Esso oil depot. The elevated road is the M6 motorway. 8 July 1984. John Turner photo

Another Sunday diversion of a Tunstead - Northwich stone train, this time 20162 + 164 with a loaded working at Denton on the Guide Bridge-Stockport line. The route taken was Tunstead-New Mills South Junction-Romiley-Guide Bridge-Denton-Stockport-Edgeley Junction-Northenden Junction instead of directly between New Mills South Junction and Northenden Junction. At the time there was a Sunday passenger service of seven trains each way between Stockport and Stalybridge but only from late afternoon onwards and none stopped at the intermediate stations including Denton. 16 September 1984

West Coast main line diversions could take several different routes in the Manchester area. From 2 September to 28 October trains left the main line at Preston and took the route through Chorley, Bolton, Victoria and Ashton Moss to Stockport. The 09.10 Glasgow Central-Poole with 47537 + 87002 is seen passing one of the magnificent semaphore signal gantries at Bolton. The semaphores were taken out of use a little over a year later in December 1985 when Burnden Junction signal box closed. 23 September 1984

This is the most obscure diversion in the book and involves the maze of lines around Guide Bridge. In October 1984 the Stockport to Stalybridge passenger service – which at that time ran Monday to Saturday and Sunday evenings – was impacted by closure of the line in the Guide Bridge station area for a month due to engineering work which included remodelling Stockport Junction. The Denton Junction-Stalybridge part of the service was diverted via Ashton Moss South Junction, OA & GB Junction and Ashton-under-Lyne, missing out Guide Bridge station. The eastern side of the Ashton Moss triangle, although technically open at the time, rarely saw trains so this was a rare event. Here we see the 11.23 Stalybridge-Stockport, formed of 52045/51930, passing the signal box at Ashton Moss South Junction. Notice that the signal box windows are being cleaned (see the ladder) and the cleaner is taking a break at the top of the steps. The signal box was closed in September 1991. All traces of the railway have since disappeared with the area behind the signal box occupied by a large Sainsbury's supermarket. 1 October 1984

Diversions of traffic from the West Coast main line over the Settle & Carlisle line have been a regular feature over the years but in the mid-1980s when closure was being threatened, they were mainly just on Sunday morning and early afternoon. In Spring 1985, several full weekends were organised which featured a decent line-up of workings. 47674 passes through Kirby Stephen with the 08.55 Euston-Glasgow Central. 6 April 1985

The very scenic central section of the Settle & Carlisle tends to get visited most often by enthusiasts with other locations being less popular. Despite a good volume of trains on that day, Long Meg Sidings signal box was switched out as 47305 passed at the head of the up Royal Scot (09.10 Glasgow Central to Euston). The signal box closed officially in 1990. As 47305 is a freight locomotive not fitted with electric train supply, the passengers in their luxurious Mark 3 coaches will have been without heating and air conditioning. 4 May 1985

A rare West Coast main line diversion occurred in spring 1985. A couple of Sunday morning trains from Birmingham New Street to Manchester Piccadilly were diverted via the freight only Warrington to Skelton Junction line. The line closed just two months later in July 1985. Here we see 47453 working the 08.32 Birmingham New Street-Manchester Piccadilly past the signal box at Lymm. Regular passenger services on the line were withdrawn in 1962. 5 May 1985

East Coast Main Line trains to and from Scotland have often been diverted at weekends via the Newcastle-Carlisle line before heading north and reaching Edinburgh by reversing at Carstairs. In pre-electrification days, most trains were formed of HSTs so assisting locomotives were not required. 43156 leads the diverted 10.25 King's Cross-Aberdeen into Cowran cutting (between Brampton and Wetheral). 43053 is on the rear. Of particular interest here are the telegraph poles and wires which, although once ubiquitous on Britain's railways, were rare by 1988. 9 April 1988. (Brian Carter)

On Sunday 17 April 1988, Trans Pennine trains were diverted after Manchester Victoria via the Calder Valley route and Halifax to Bradford Interchange. Here they reversed to reach Leeds which involved the locomotive running round its coaches. The normal route for this train from Manchester Victoria across the Pennines would be via the Diggle route, Huddersfield and Dewsbury to Leeds, avoiding Bradford completely. 47652 leaves Bradford Exchange with the 13.50 Liverpool Lime Street-Newcastle. 17 April 1988. (John Turner)

For much of the late '80s, diversions were scheduled for West Coast services when the main line between Wigan North Western and Euxton Junction (south of Preston) was closed for engineering work. The diversionary route via the Bolton line as far as Lostock Junction was operationally awkward because it involved reversal at both Wigan North Western and Lostock Junction. The solution was to add an extra locomotive (or pair) to the rear of the train and run it in top-and-tailed formation to Lostock Junction where reversal could take place. Many of these workings used a pair of Class 20s as the extra locomotives. 20172 and 20028 work the 13.30 Preston-Euston away from Lostock Junction towards Wigan with 47503 on rear. 29 January 1989. (Stewart Jolly)

On several weekends in early 1989, Cross Country trains were diverted north of Birmingham. Their normal route was from Birmingham New Street to Wolverhampton and Stafford but instead they were diverted via Walsall and the Cannock line to Rugeley. At the time, the Cannock line was freight only but a passenger service to Hednesford was introduced on 10 April 1989. Rebuilding work is in progress as 47449 passes the site of Hednesford station with the 15.10 Birmingham New Street-Manchester Piccadilly. 26 February 1989. (Antony Guppy)

47624 leads the diverted 08.35 Birmingham New Street-Llandudno through Cannock Chase Forest at Marquis's Drive. Regular passenger services on this stretch of line were introduced in June 1997, extending the re-introduced service to Hednesford which started the day after this picture was taken. The foot crossing here has since been replaced by a footbridge suitable for the many horses and off-road cyclists using the forest. Electrification through to Rugeley was completed in December 2018. 9 April 1989. (Antony Guppy)

In 1989, a full programme of Settle & Carlisle diversions operated for several spring weekends when the West Coast main line over Shap was closed for engineering work. Although all the diverted passenger trains were worked by Class 47 diesels, the working shown here featured a freight locomotive without electrical train supply. 47365 passes Settle Junction with the 12.37 Glasgow Central-Euston. The Motorail van immediately behind the locomotive is an unusual sight on an express passenger train. 11 March 1989

During these weekends, several steel trains from Mossend to Margam were diverted over the Carnforth to Settle Junction line via Clapham as their weight and low speed meant they could not be accommodated with the passenger trains on the Settle & Carlisle. At Settle Junction 20028 + 172 on a Mossend-Margam steel train crawls up to the signal while 47527 working the 10.25 Glasgow Central-Euston passes at speed on the main line. 11 March 1989

The steel trains ran close together. 20120 and 20090 with steel coils destined for Margam Yard have been given a clear signal to pass Settle Junction and head for Hellifield. At this time, freight traffic was unusual on the Carnforth-Settle line. The steel originated from Ravenscraig steelworks which closed in 1992. The new town of Ravenscraig now occupies the site. 11 March 1989

At dusk, 47436 on the 13.00 Euston-Glasgow Central crosses Ribblehead viaduct. Class 47 locomotives have a distinctive smoky exhaust which is clearly visible in this picture. The Settle to Carlisle route is double track throughout except across this viaduct and a 20mph speed restriction applies. The viaduct is also Grade II listed. A month after this picture was taken, the line was reprieved from closure by the Transport Minister, Michael Portillo. 11 March 1989

During most weekend diversions it was unusual to see a freight train, but one ran north along the Leamside line on the Sunday afternoon. 47231 heads a long rake of vans containing petfood forming a Wisbech-Deanside working which is seen approaching the automatic half barrier level crossing at Follingsby, just south of Pelaw. At the time, this train was a regular Sunday runner on its normal route along the East Coast Main Line through Durham. 12 March 1989

Diverted passenger trains, mostly formed of HSTs, ran roughly hourly in each direction which made pathing interesting on the single track section between Washington and Penshaw over Penshaw Viaduct. An HST bound for King's Cross with 43104 leading passes the coal loader under construction on the site of Follingsby Colliery. The loader was built to serve Wardley opencast colliery and had a short life, closing in the 1990s. When the coal industry was privatised in 1995, Wardley passed to RJB Mining and was eventually closed in 2005. The Leamside line itself, apart from the section serving the coal loader, closed in 1991. 12 March 1989

Sunday diversions of Liverpool trains between Runcorn and Crewe via Chester were fairly common in the 1980s and '90s. Timings in the Summer 1990 timetable allowed diversions from 5 August to the end of the timetable on 30 September. With Halton Junction signal box visible in the distance, 47425 leaves Runcorn on the Halton curve towards Frodsham while working the 13.02 Liverpool Lime St-Euston. Reversal at Chester normally involved turning the whole train via the Northgate triangle rather than running the loco round in the station. The line here was singled and de-electrified in 1994. 16 September 1990. (Stewart Jolly)

A programme of diversions over the full length of the former Great Northern & Great Eastern Joint Line was organised for three weekends in February 1991 while engineering work took place on various crossovers and tunnels on the East Coast main line. They were blighted by bad weather and eventually abandoned. On the first weekend, 47517, with a DVT on the 07.40 Leeds-King's Cross, approaches Spalding station. This location has changed enormously over the years with the extensive sidings on the left being lifted and the land subsequently sold off for housing. The sidings on the right were brought back into use in 2020 for a flow of calcium carbonate from Aberdeen which was destined for a paper company in Kings Lynn. Sadly, the traffic ceased after a few months when the paper company changed suppliers. 2 February 1991

Another view of the 07.40 Leeds-King's Cross passing through Spalding, this time showing 91020 on the rear. The area to the right of the train was once completely covered by sidings and running lines. Today the siding on the left has been removed, the station has just two platforms and the area in the background is occupied by a housing estate and many tall trees. See the pictures on page 109. 2 February 1991

47594 works the 10.10 Leeds-King's Cross past Gosberton. On this day, only the Leeds trains featured Class 91 sets hauled by Class 47s. All others were HSTs. Since the 1982 picture on Page 14 was taken, the goods loop and telegraph poles have been removed. Although the locomotive is allocated to the Railfreight Metals Sector, it has electrical train supply to power the heating on the coaches. The semaphore signals survived until Gosberton signal box was replaced in 2012. 2 February 1991

An HST working the 09.10 Glasgow Central-King's Cross approaches the signal box at Blotoft, south of Sleaford. This signal box was in a remote location, Helpringham Fen, miles from the nearest village of Helpringham. The adjacent level crossing was too awkward to be automated in the 1980s and '90s, so the signal box here outlived its neighbour at Helpringham which, in its final years, was simply a block post. Closure of the signal box came in 2014 when the whole line was re-signalled to a new signalling centre in Lincoln. There is no nearby place called Blotoft. The name only appears on a local farm. 2 February 1991

On the 1992 May Bank Holiday, closure of the WCML for engineering work saw an hourly replacement service run on the Midland Main Line between St. Pancras and Liverpool Lime Street. Class 47 diesel haulage was used from Nuneaton southwards with the electric loco taking over at Bedford on many trains for the run into London using power from the 25kV electrification. Wearing the simplified version of Rail Express Systems livery, 47635 passes rows of stored HEA and HAA coal hoppers in the sidings of the former Wellingborough motive power depot, working the 17.10 St. Pancras-Liverpool Lime Street. 86229 is on the rear and will take over at Nuneaton. 23 May 1992. (Antony Guppy)

Inter-City liveried 47813 with matching coaching stock sweeps through the speed restricted reverse curves at Market Harborough station while working the 10.10 St. Pancras-Liverpool Lime Street. With the growth in long distance commuting, a very large additional car park has since been built on the land in the foreground. Despite the electric locomotive remaining attached, some trains were worked by their diesel loco all the way through to St. Pancras. 25 May 1992. (Antony Guppy)

On Sundays up to mid-afternoon in the latter part of the summer 1992 timetable (from 12 July to 27 September), Liverpool-Euston services were diverted via Manchester Piccadilly. This involved trains taking the non-electrified line via Huyton, Earlestown and Eccles before branching off to Oxford Road and Piccadilly at Ordsall Lane Junction. 47557 leads the 10.55 Liverpool Lime St-Euston at Hough Green. The attractive station building dates from 1874 and is Grade II listed. 27 September 1992

47584 passes through Sankey station with the 12.55 Liverpool Lime St-Euston, also running via Manchester. 87028 is just out of sight on the rear. The station building, a standard design by the Cheshire Lines Committee, is undergoing roof repair. The building has survived but sees a token train service of two trains per day each way as it is overshadowed by Warrington West station half a mile to the east which was opened in 2019. 27 September 1992

On the 1993 August Bank Holiday weekend, the West Coast main line was closed in the Warrington area and through trains were diverted. Here we see 47971 at St Helens Central working the 15.15 Preston-Euston. The route for this train involved diesel haulage from Preston with reversal at Liverpool Lime Street station to provide a passenger service to Euston. 87012 is the electric locomotive on the rear. 28 August 1993. (Antony Guppy)

An unusual feature of this weekend was a diverted freight train which kept its electric locomotive in the formation. 47350 tows 90036 through St. Helens Junction station with the 21.35 Aberdeen Guild Street-Willesden. The train has travelled southwards along the West Coast Main Line and turned off at Golbourne Junction before heading west towards Liverpool. It will reverse direction at Edge Hill sidings before it can head south via Runcorn. The large building on the right is the remains of Bold B power station which closed in 1991. 28 August 1993. (Antony Guppy)

The South Western main line to Southampton was closed for engineering work during the weekend of 20/21 May 1995 and a few freightliner trains were diverted via Andover, Salisbury Laverstock Curve and Romsey. 47210 works a Lawley Street-Southampton liner past the ground frame at East Grimstead. The siding here served a quarry which had been disused for many years. The red logo on the side of the locomotive shows that it belongs to Railfreight Distribution. 20 May 1995

During the weekend of 13/14 January 1996, the South Western main line to Southampton was closed for engineering work with both cross country passenger and freight trains diverted via Andover, Salisbury Laverstock Curve and Romsey. 47520 approaches Romsey station with a Southampton-Lawley Street liner. This was an Inter-City locomotive operating a freight train which, although not completely unknown in the days of British Rail, was unusual. This practice would become less common when rail privatisation started a month later. The line to the left goes to Eastleigh. 13 January 1996

For the whole of the weekend 18/19 May 1996 the West Coast main line between Carlisle and Glasgow was closed with trains being diverted via the former Glasgow & South Western route. The first down train on the Saturday morning was 47763 hauling the 23.55 Euston-Glasgow Central sleeper, seen on the curve near Park. This was a particularly smoky locomotive which left a trail of fumes lingering in the air for several minutes after passing. 18 May 1996

In glorious evening sunshine, the 11.19 Bournemouth-Glasgow Central HST led by 43088 passes Thornhill signal box. The austere appearance of the brick built signal box is due to it being an Air Raid Precautions design dating from 1943 which was intended to resist blast damage from bombs. On this day the passenger trains were roughly hourly with occasional freight trains. A loop was opened in the 2000s to support freight traffic (mainly coal) which has since ceased to run. 18 May 1996

On the same weekend, one of the diverted freight trains is seen here. 37116 + 026 head north at Mennock, south of Sanquhar with a Carlisle-Mossend freight. Of interest are the wagons behind the locos carrying pipes and the large number of wagons carrying coal in containers. The sign clearly shows the adjacent A76 road which has since bypassed the location on a new alignment and the old A76 has become a small farm access road. 18 May 1996

47839 with the 12.30 Glasgow-Poole approaches New Cumnock. The station here had been closed in 1965 but was reopened in 1991. The signal box dates from 1909 and with the resurgence of Scottish coal in the early 2000s, its area of control was expanded to include Greenburn Junction and the line to the nearby open cast colliery. With coal burning by power stations being phased out in the UK, the coal traffic has ceased. 18 May 1996

Rail privatisation led to GNER taking over the franchise for the East Coast Main Line. They understood the need for continuing services during periods of engineering work rather than putting passengers on buses and organised a series of diversions from 1997 until their demise in 2007. The line through Yarm had been freight only until the previous year when a station was opened on the south side of the town and a local passenger service started. On Easter Saturday 1997, 47775 heads south over Yarm Viaduct with the 14.45 Glasgow Central-King's Cross. 29 March 1997

47785 passes through Stockton station with the 12.45 Glasgow Central-King's Cross. 91013 is out of sight on the rear. On this the weekend, the diversions were between Northallerton and Ferryhill through Eaglescliffe and Stockton with the pilot diesel locomotives mostly being attached or removed at Newcastle and Northallerton. The sidings in the foreground lead to the T.J. Thomson scrapyard which was the final destination for many locomotives and items of railway rolling stock over the years and closed in 2017. 30 March 1997

Freight trains supplying the Welsh steel industry have typically run every day of the week including Sundays. When engineering work closed, the Welsh main line at Easter 1997 it was decided to route the steel trains via a long diversion over the Central Wales line. 56073 + 56064 cross Cynghordy Viaduct (6 miles north east of Llandovery) with a diverted Margam-Ebbw Vale train carrying steel coils to make tinplate. Sadly, the Ebbw Vale tinplate works closed in 2002. 30 March 1997. (John Turner)

The journey of the diverted trains from Margam yard involved taking the single-track Central Wales line from Hendy Junction to Craven Arms where they reversed, then travelling via Hereford, Abergavenny and Newport. The Central Wales line normally sees just four passenger trains per day each way and no freights. Knighton is a crossing point on the line where 37894 + 37704 are seen with a diverted Margam-Llanwern train carrying steel slabs. 30 March 1997. (John Turner)

On the 1997 Whitsun Bank Holiday, GNER operated East Coast main line diversions from Doncaster to Newark via Gainsborough and Lincoln. An unusual mix of Class 47s was hired from EWS to tow the Class 91 sets comprising some previously used by RES and a couple of former BR Research Department locos. 47972 in BR Technical Services livery heads west near Park Drain crossing (east of Finningley near Doncaster) with 91031 on the 12.00 King's Cross-Glasgow Central. 25 May 1997

An unusual sight for a Sunday was 56003 in Loadhaul livery with an empty steel train at Park Drain level crossing. There were no freight trains timetabled on the main line on Sundays and steel trains were not routed this way on any day so it must have been a diversion of some kind. It could have been an additional Immingham-Tinsley working running via Lincoln instead of taking the usual Scunthorpe route. One of the 30 locomotives built in Romania by Electroputere, 56003 survived into preservation after being withdrawn from service. It was then purchased by Devon & Cornwall Railways (DCR), renumbered 56312 and put back into traffic. In 2018 it was bought by Gbrf as a reserve candidate for rebuilding into a Class 69. 25 May 1997

Former departmental locomotive 47976 in civil engineers' livery working the 09.06 Edinburgh Waverley-King's Cross passes the old goods shed at Haxey and Epworth station which closed to passengers in 1959. Adjacent to this station, Haxey Junction was the southern terminus of the short-lived Isle of Axholme Joint Railway which opened in 1905, closed to passengers in 1933 and completely in 1956. The railway ran to Goole via Crowle and the main traffic flow was peat. 25 May 1997

Viewed through a powerful telephoto lens, GNER's 09.40 Inverness-King's Cross approaches the level crossing and signal box at Stow Park, between Gainsborough and Saxilby. At this time GNER had been operating for a little over a year and only the power cars have been repainted into their dark blue livery while the coaches remain in BR Inter-City livery. The semaphore signals here were replaced and the signal box, dating from 1876, closed after re-signalling in 2013. 25 May 1997

After rail privatisation, Virgin Trains took over services on the West Coast Main Line and continued the practice of diverting Euston to Wolverhampton services via Nuneaton instead of the direct route via Coventry. These continued regularly over selected weekends for the next ten years, sometimes all weekend and on other occasions just part of a Sunday. In summer 1997, they took place every Sunday between 3 August and 21 September. 47749 towing 87008 leaves Nuneaton past the site of Abbey Junction with the 10.45 Euston-Wolverhampton. 10 August 1997

Cross country services were sometimes diverted over the Nuneaton-Water Orton line as well. 47807 leads the 09.00 Manchester Piccadilly-Poole past Whitacre Junction. The normal route would have been Stafford-Wolverhampton-Birmingham New Street whereas the route taken on this day was Stafford-Nuneaton-Water Orton-Birmingham New Street with reversal at Nuneaton. The locomotive carries an unusual purple and white livery that had been applied earlier in the year to two of the Class 47s owned by Porterbook Leasing – 47807 and 47817. 10 August 1997

East Coast Main Line services in the north east of England were diverted via Eaglescliffe and the Durham Coast line on the Sunday of the 1997 August Bank Holiday weekend. HST 43091 operated by Virgin Cross Country passes Billingham signal box with what would normally be the 10.15 Newcastle-Plymouth but which had been retimed to depart earlier to maintain booked timings later in the journey. The pair of semaphore signal arms on the left indicate a junction: the main route is the Durham coast line to Seaham and Sunderland while the route diverging to the right is the freight only line to Belasis Lane and Seal Sands. 24 August 1997

When first introduced in 1995, Eurostar services started at Waterloo International station and ran to the Channel Tunnel on the third rail 750V DC system via Orpington, Sevenoaks, Tonbridge and Ashford. On those occasions when the main line through Tonbridge was closed for engineering work, they were diverted via Swanley, Otford and Maidstone East before re-joining their normal route at Ashford. 3013 and 3012 curve through Eynsford station with the 09.10 Paris Gare du Nord-Waterloo International. 1 February 1998. (Antony Guppy)

At Easter 1998 the East Coast Main Line through Durham was closed all weekend and diversions operated via the scenic Durham Coast line. A small number of freight trains were diverted in addition to GNER and Virgin Cross Country passenger trains. Saturday 12 April started out cold with a sprinkling of snow on the ground as EWS's 60097, still in Transrail livery, leaves Hartlepool with a Hardendale-Lackenby working. The wagons are carrying limestone for use in steel making on Teeside. The signal box to the rear of the train is Stranton which was closed in 2010. 12 April 1998

With a particularly dirty exhaust, 47733 passes the former junction at Hart, north of Hartlepool, working the 11.00 Edinburgh-King's Cross. On the left is the track bed of the line built by Hartlepool Dock and Railway company from Hartlepool to Haswell which was opened in 1832 and closed in 1964. The coast line from Seaham, which the train has just taken, was a late addition to the railway network, opening in 1905. 12 April 1998

All the locomotive hauled trains this weekend used former RES Class 47s hired in from EWS. 47792 hauls 91022 on the 10.45 Glasgow Central-King's Cross past the allotments at Horden. Until its closure in 1987, Horden Colliery was situated in the background to the left of the railway. A new station opened here in June 2020, built in just six months, to serve Horden and the adjacent town of Peterlee. 12 April 1998

GNER's 43117 leads the 13.30 King's Cross-Aberdeen through the former Monkwearmouth station which closed in 1967. On the left is Monkwearmouth railway museum, based in the old station building, which opened in 1973 and closed in 2017. The museum has since re-opened dedicated to football. The railway here is now electrified and carries Tyne & Wear Metro trains on the line to South Hylton. 12 April 1998

GNER diverted trains via Lincoln on the 1998 May Day and August Bank Holidays, on both occasions beginning on the Saturday early evening. GNER HST 43117 + 113 passes Gainsborough Lea Road with the 09.50 Aberdeen-King's Cross. Despite trains sometimes being held up by others in front due to the increased traffic resulting from the diversions, the signal box was switched out on this day. After being damaged by fire in 2009 it was no longer operational and closed officially in 2014 when the line between Lincoln and Gainsborough Trent Junction was re-signalled. 3 May 1998

47736 crosses the River Trent at Gainsborough Trent Junction with the 15.00 King's Cross-Edinburgh Waverley and is about to diverge to the right on the line to Doncaster. The line to the left goes to Retford. The semaphore signals here lasted until re-signalling of the line to Lincoln in 2014 with the nearby signal box just out of the shot to the right being retained as a fringe box to Lincoln Signalling Centre. 3 May 1998

47739 rounds the curve on the west side of Lincoln with the 09.30 Newcastle-King's Cross. This section of line was opened in 1985 to connect the Newark line with West Holmes Junction on the line through Lincoln Central station, allowing all passenger trains to serve Central station and St Marks station to be closed. A single track connecting spur from Boultham Junction to Pyewipe Junction following the course of the old Lincoln avoiding line allows trains such this one to run directly between Newark and Saxilby. 30 August 1998

Class 91 locomotives were built to work with sets of Mark 4 coaches and a DVT (Driving Van Trailer) with the sloping end of the locomotive normally facing north at King's Cross. Nevertheless, the locomotives also had a cab at each end with the inner end cab – usually called the blunt end by enthusiasts – intended for exceptional occasions when the main cab could not be used. Here is the rare sight of the blunt end of 91027 on the rear of the 09.00 Edinburgh Waverley-King's Cross as it passes Saxilby. 30 August 1998

In the summers of 1998 and 1999, D9000 was hired to Virgin Cross Country to operate their summer Saturdays-only train to Ramsgate. The train would normally take the line from Birmingham New Street to London via Coventry and Rugby but on this occasion, due to engineering work, all trains to London were diverted via Water Orton to join the West Coast Main Line at Nuneaton. With an exceptionally smoky exhaust, D9000 accelerates past Washwood Heath No 1 signal box (barely visible behind the second coach) with the 06.58 from Birmingham New Street to Ramsgate. The train terminated at Margate on this day due to late running following a half hour delay at Nuneaton and returned north on the 11.38 ex-Margate. 18 July 1998

Birmingham to Euston diversions via Nuneaton took place on the weekend of 18/19 July 1998 and Virgin Trains hired in a varied set of Class 47 locomotives including freight locomotives. 47703 was hired from Fragonset Railways and leads the 18.19 Wolverhampton-Euston past Whitacre Junction. The large building to the left of the train is the pumping station at Whitacre Waterworks, built in 1883 to supply water to Birmingham from nearby Shustoke Reservoir and now Grade II listed. Today it supplies water to Coventry. 18 July 1998

It was rare to see double headed Class 47 haulage on any diversions. In this picture at Castle Bromwich EWS's 47355 and Fragonset's 47703 haul 86233 on the 08.35 Euston-Wolverhampton. The Class 47s took over the train at Nuneaton. 47355 looks on the outside to be in a rundown state and survived only until early 1999 when it was put into store. On the loop line on the left can be seen a surviving platform from Castle Bromwich station which closed in 1968. 18 July 1998

Freight locomotive 47219, formerly used by Railfreight Distribution, passes the station and disused signal box at Water Orton with the 10.19 Wolverhampton-Euston. At the time, the signal box was used as an office. Dating from 1963 and built to a standard BR London Midland Region design, it replaced an older signal box that had been damaged by a derailed freight train. Its working life was short as it was replaced by Saltley Power Signal box in 1969. 18 July 1998

In late December 1998 and early January 1999, the Bristol-Gloucester main line was closed with Virgin Cross Country trains diverted via Lydney and Newport where the trains reversed. 47806 approaches Pilning with the 06.40 York-Bristol Temple Meads having just left the Severn Tunnel. The approach to the second Severn Bridge can be seen in the background. 47806 carried on working for Virgin until 2002 and was rebuilt into 57309 in 2003. 9 January 1999

The Midland Main Line to the south of Leicester was closed on Sundays for much of the 1998/9 winter timetable with an hourly service of trains to and from St Pancras diverted via Melton Mowbray and Corby. Operated by Midland Mainline, 43064 + 082 approach Melton Mowbray with the 11.30 St Pancras-Sheffield. Trains still served Leicester station which meant that they had to traverse the single track spur line between Syston South and East Junctions and reverse at Leicester. 10 January 1999

Midland Mainline's 10.13 Derby-St Pancras with 43055 + 083 in charge has been diverted and is seen on the line from Corby at Glendon Junction re-joining the main line. This is the same location as the picture on page 15 but with the key difference that the Corby line is single track. The singling was carried out during re-signalling in 1987. In 2020 the line was rebuilt to be double track again and electrified as far as Corby. 7 February 1999

A Midland Mainline HST forming the 09.43 Leeds-St Pancras passes through rolling Rutland countryside near the village of Seaton. The train has just crossed Seaton Viaduct and the track bed of the branch line from Seaton to Uppingham which closed in 1960. It is between the Glaston and Seaton Tunnels and will soon cross the famous 82-arch Welland Viaduct at Harringworth which is the longest masonry viaduct in the country. 7 February 1999

During early 1999, the Great Western main line between Didcot and Swindon was closed for several Saturdays for engineering work. Trains from London to Bristol and South Wales were diverted via Westbury, the Avon Valley and Bath. Great Western's 43177 leads the 09.55 Bristol Temple Meads-Paddington at Bradford Junction. The single track in the background runs through Melksham to Thingley Junction near Chippenham. Since 1999, a housing estate has been built on the fields on the right. 16 January 1999

43149 + 187 in the green and white Great Western livery approach Freshford with the 13.30 Paddington-Swansea. During these diversions there were broadly two diverted HSTs per hour in each direction. The train operating company had just rebranded itself as First Great Western and introduced a new livery which was a variation of the livery shown here. The First Group logo replaced the Great Western logo, and a large gold stripe was added to the white area on the lower half of all the vehicles. 16 January 1999

One of the more unusual diversions involved Virgin Cross Country services to the South Coast which would normally take the direct Coventry-Birmingham New Street line. On this Sunday they were diverted via the Coventry-Nuneaton and then Nuneaton-Water Orton-Birmingham New Street lines. 47709, hired to Virgin from Fragonset Railways, leads the 11.13 Manchester Piccadilly-Southampton at Three Spires Junction. The disused lines on the left which once lead to Coventry Colliery and the Coventry Homefire Coking Plant were subsequently reopened to a new Prologis Park distribution terminal and controlled from a panel in a new portacabin. Unfortunately, the lines became disused again when the Evian bottled water traffic was switched to Daventry International Railfreight Terminal in 2007. 24 January 1999

47827 passes the remains of Three Spires Junction signal box with the 10.34 Southampton Central-Manchester Piccadilly. The signal box had been destroyed in an arson attack a few months previously although the sidings it controlled were already out of use. This line was freight only from 1965 (when intermediate stations were closed) until 1988 when Bedworth station was re-opened and a local passenger service started. In 2002, 47827 was rebuilt with new major components to become 57302 which appears on Page 72. 24 January 1999

During spring 1999, West Coast Main Line services were diverted over the Settle & Carlisle line for several Saturdays. With snow patches on the crags of Wild Boar Fell in the background, Virgin Cross Country HST power cars 43078 + 093 head south in a patch of sunshine at Ais Gill with the 11.10 Glasgow Central-Penzance. This is the highest point on the Settle-Carlisle route, 1169 feet (356m) above sea level. 13 March 1999

47840 rounds the curve at Garsdale towards the station with the 09.10 Edinburgh Waverley-Brighton operated by Virgin Cross Country. Out of sight in the foreground is the disused track bed of the line to Hawes which was closed in 1959. 47840 stayed working with Virgin through to the end of loco hauled cross country services, being repainted into BR blue livery in May 2002 and working the last train double headed with 47847 on 19 August 2002. 13 March 1999

47703, hired from Fragonset Railways, passes through Blackburn station with the 06.55 Birmingham New St-Edinburgh Waverley. This was the first northbound diverted train on that day, passing at 09.26. It will soon enter Blackburn Tunnel, then turn left at Daisyfield Junction on to the line to Hellifield and Settle Junction. Diverted trains were roughly hourly in each direction. The impressive station roof was removed when the station was refurbished in 2000. 20 March 1999

Services on the West Coast Main Line to and from the south need to reverse at Preston to get to the Settle & Carlisle line. 47818 rounds the Lostock Curve to the south of Preston as it heads towards Blackburn after reversal with the 09.15 Bristol Temple Meads-Edinburgh Waverley. At the rear of the train is the junction for the single track branch line to Ormskirk. 47818 was sold to Cotswold Rail in 2003 and appears on page 77 in One livery. 20 March 1999

A very unusual feature of this set of diversions was that one Virgin Cross Country train in each direction was routed over the Blackburn-Bolton line. D9000 was used as a pilot on the southbound Cross Country service and in this picture we see it with 47844 passing the back streets of Blackburn on the single track line towards Darwen. The working is the 09.10 Edinburgh Waverley-Brighton and the Deltic's headcode panel displays the train's actual headcode. 20 March 1999

The northbound diverted service is seen from above Sough Tunnel between Bolton and Darwen as it heads towards Blackburn with the 05.50 Bournemouth-Glasgow Central. Taking this route saved time as the usual route via the West Coast main line was longer and involved a reversal at Preston. The locomotive is 47709 which was owned at the time by Fragonset Railways and hired to Virgin. Normally this line only saw diesel units as the last freight service carrying oil to Reed Paper at Darwen ceased running in the early 1990s. 20 March 1999

On Easter Saturday and Sunday 1999, the Durham Coast line was again used for diversions away from the East Coast Main Line through Durham. Surrounded by a typical north eastern fog from the sea, 47777 brings 91009 round the sharp curve through Hartlepool station with the 06.05 King's Cross-Edinburgh Waverley. Only one bi-directional platform is used by stopping passenger trains even though the line here is double track. The platform on the left and roof supports over the tracks have since been removed. 3 April 1999

Virgin Cross Country trains were diverted as well as GNER. Virgin's 43098 + 43013 head north at Norton with the 06.22 Plymouth-Newcastle. The train will pass four closely spaced signal boxes in a little over two miles. It has already passed the Norton South and Norton East signal boxes on the Norton triangle and will soon pass Norton-on-Tees and Billingham. All survived until re-signalling in 2021. 3 April 1999

47761 works the 12.00 Edinburgh-King's Cross through Norton on the outskirts of Stockton-on-Tees with 91004 at the rear of the train. The very tall signal box in the background, Norton-on-Tees, was opened in 1897 and controlled a level crossing. On this day, the service of GNER trains was hourly in each direction, formed mostly of Class 91 electric sets (hauled by a Class 47 diesel) with the remainder HST worked plus some additional long distance services formed of HSTs. 3 April 1999

GNER HST power cars 43119 + 43108 run southwards beside Embankment Road at Seaham with the 10.30 Edinburgh Waverley-King's Cross, the only HST operated Edinburgh Waverley service on the day. The distinctive semaphore signal at this location was soon replaced by a much shorter and simpler signal and then removed completely in 2010 when the area was re-signalled. The old siding behind the train has also been removed. 4 April 1999

In summer 1999, the Nuneaton diversions took place every Sunday for the whole of the day from the start of the timetable on 30 May to 18 July. 47575 tows the 09.59 Wolverhampton-Euston through open countryside near Water Orton. At this point the train is crossing a bridge over the River Tame and is also on one side of the triangular junction for the freight-only line to Ryecroft Junction which can just be seen above the foreground trees on the right of the picture. 11 July 1999

On Sunday, 8 August 1999, Virgin West Coast and Cross Country trains to and from Glasgow were diverted via the Glasgow and South Western line through Kilmarnock and Dumfries. 47848 hauls 86212 and the 09.29 Glasgow Central-Plymouth near Park. This train is formed of Mark 2 coaches like all normal Cross Country services. Use of Mark 3 coaches with a DVT on Cross Country only happened on exceptional occasions. 8 August 1999

On Saturday and Sunday 22/23 April 2000, engineering work at Oxford meant that some Virgin Cross Country trains between Birmingham and the south coast were diverted via the West Coast Main Line. 43123 + 43063 are seen on Acton Bank with the 06.50 Edinburgh Waverley-Bournemouth being passed by a Class 332 Heathrow Express unit heading to the airport. The leading power car 43123 is one of eight in service with Virgin that had conventional buffers and couplings. These power cars were used as Driving Van Trailers (DVTs) during commissioning of Class 91s in 1988 and fitted with buffers to facilitate shunting as the production DVTs were not yet ready for traffic. 22 April 2000

On the weekend of 30 April/1 May 2000, GNER diverted their King's Cross services between Wakefield Westgate and Leeds via the non-electrified route through Wakefield Kirkgate, Normanton and Woodlesford. This involved reversal when the Class 47 picked up the train at Wakefield Westgate. 47786 + 90025 approach Normanton working the diverted 18.14 Leeds-King's Cross. Use of a Class 90 hired from EWS in place of the usual GNER Class 91 was unusual. 30 April 2000. (John Turner)

47781 + 91112 pass Holbeck (to the south of central Leeds) working the 13.44 Leeds-London King's Cross, diverted via Normanton. The Class 91 electric locomotive would normally be at the north end of the train but because of the reversal at Wakefield Kirkgate, it is at the south end. Holbeck motive power depot was situated on the left just beyond the bridge in the background. The distinctive red brick building on the right was built in 1901 as Holbeck public library and had several uses after the library was moved including being a pub. It was converted into offices and Grade II listed in 1996. The ugly modern warehouse building behind it was demolished in 2008. 1 May 2000. (John Turner)

As happened in 1998 and 1999, East Coast Main Line diversions via Newark and Lincoln operated on the Sunday and Monday of the August Bank Holiday weekend in 2000. Swinderby has a good set of semaphore signals and some are visible in this view of 47759 with the 08.00 Edinburgh Waverley-King's Cross approaching the level crossing and station. The signal box is due to be replaced during re-signalling in 2022. 27 August 2000

EWS liveried 47785 working the 09.00 Edinburgh Waverley-King's Cross passes a superb lattice post semaphore distant signal north of Saxilby. This was my favourite signal on the line. It used to be a home signal operated by Sykes Junction signal box but following its closure in September 1988 the home arm was removed. The distant arm remained in use controlled by Saxilby signal box. Due to the distance involved, the arm was worked by an electric motor rather than the usual cable and made a wonderful whirring noise when it operated. 27 August 2000

47775 with the 17.15 Newcastle-King's Cross rounds the sharp curve from Trent Junction into Gainsborough Lea Road station. In the background on the left the coal-fired West Burton 'A' power station, which first generated power in 1966, is working at half load with four of its eight cooling towers in use. On the right is the terminal which sent oil from local wells by train for refining and which closed three years previously in 1997. 27 August 2000

On Saturday 17 February 2001 the Great Western main line through Swindon was closed and both passenger and freight trains were diverted via the Berks & Hants line through Westbury. An empty coal train from Didcot to Avonmouth Docks is seen near Aldermaston with 60003 in charge. The coal fired Didcot A power station closed in 2013, leaving the smaller gas-powered Didcot B still operating. The wagons are the once ubiquitous 4-wheel HAA coal hoppers which were replaced by high-capacity HTA bogie hoppers from 2001 onwards. They became extinct on the UK rail network by 2010 although many were rebuilt with new bodies for infrastructure use. 17 February 2001

47817 leads the 08.08 Manchester Piccadilly-Poole Virgin Cross Country service through Wokingham and takes the line to Guildford. The South Western main line through Winchester was closed for engineering work and these long distance trains were diverted via Guildford and Havant to re-join the main line at St Denys. Worthy of note here are the mechanical Southern Railway shunt signals near the front of the loco and on the right on top of a post which survived even though the main running signals at the time were colour lights. 18 February 2001

Virgin Cross Country 47827 passes Barrow Hill working the 09.05 Birmingham New Street-Newcastle. Due to engineering work between Chesterfield and Sheffield the train has been diverted via the 'Old Road' which is normally freight only. It will travel via Beighton Junction, Woodhouse Junction and Woodburn Junction before entering Sheffield station from the north. The locomotive will then run round its train to reverse direction before departing for York and Newcastle. 25 February 2001. (John Turner)

On 3 March 2001, engineering work in the Aylesbury area meant that the Northolt-Calvert bin liner could not take its normal route via Princes Risborough. Instead, it had to run via Greenford, Southall, Reading and Oxford to take the line via Bicester Town to Claydon where it would run round before branching off at Claydon LNE Junction to reach the unloading station at Calvert. In this view, the train is leaving Bicester with 60061 in charge. The line here became disused in 2017 after the passage of a Class 121 railtour pending reconstruction as part of the East-West route from Oxford to Bedford and Cambridge. 3 March 2001

Due to engineering work between Birmingham and Rugby, trains between Euston and Wolverhampton were diverted via Nuneaton on Sundays for the whole of the summer 2001 timetable. As usual, trains were diesel hauled between Nuneaton and Birmingham New Street. With a fully matching Virgin livery throughout, 47854 and 87020 pass Washwood Heath Yard with the 09.30 Euston-Wolverhampton. The yard is full of wagons loaded with cars from the MG Rover factory at Longbridge which closed in 2005. 24 June 2001

At Daw Mill colliery RES-liveried 86243 is seen on the rear of the 16.19 Wolverhampton-Euston with 47784 on the front behind the trees. 86243 was an EWS-owned locomotive that normally worked mail and parcel trains and was occasionally hired by Virgin to work passenger trains. The colliery was the last to operate in the Midlands and finally closed in 2013 following a severe underground fire. The whole site has now been cleared. 24 June 2001

Virgin Cross Country trains normally ran via the single track Leamington Spa-Coventry line to and from Birmingham New Street. On Sunday, 29 July 2001, these trains were diverted via Hatton and Solihull. 47827 is seen beside the M40 motorway near Hatton with the 14.18 Bournemouth-Liverpool Lime Street. Since 2001 the bushes have grown to such an extent that trains can no longer be seen from the motorway. 29 July 2001

On Sunday, 29 July 2001, 47848 failed at Bristol on the 09.08 Bristol Temple Meads-Edinburgh Waverley and 37419 was hired by Virgin to work the train as far as Birmingham New Street. 37419 was then used to pilot 47807 on the 10.15 Glasgow-Penzance from Birmingham New Street back to Bristol Temple Meads. 37419 is seen with 47807 at Droitwich Spa having been diverted over the route via Worcester as the direct route from Stoke Works Junction to Abbotswood Junction which by-passed Worcester was closed for engineering work. 29 July 2001

In summer 2002, as part of an operation known as Project Evergreen, Chiltern Railways had a two week block on their main line to reinstate double track on the single line section between Bicester North and Aynho Junction. During this time, a few through peak hour trains from the West Midlands were diverted via Oxford and Reading and ran into Paddington. 168109 + 106 pass through Langley with the 18.48 Paddington-Stourbridge. 25 April 2002

In 2002, diversions of Wolverhampton – Euston services via Nuneaton took place for the whole of the summer timetable, from 2 June to 28 September. Between 11 August and 28 September, the West Coast main line was closed between Euston and Hemel Hempstead so trains from the Rugby direction terminated at Milton Keynes. To celebrate the end of loco hauled workings, Virgin Cross Country painted several of their Class 47/8 fleet in 2001/2 in heritage liveries instead of standard Virgin livery. 47853 emerged from the paint shop in late 2001 wearing the same experimental XP64 blue livery it had carried when brand new in 1964 and numbered D1733. Here we see 47853 with 87033 at Whitacre Jn on a Wolverhampton - Milton Keynes empty stock working. 1 September 2002

Two locomotives in heritage liveries – 47847 and 86233 – are seen working the 15.26 Milton Keynes-Wolverhampton at Saltley in central Birmingham just a couple of miles from New Street station. 47847 was repainted by Virgin into BR large loco blue livery in 2001 while 86233 had been repainted just a couple of months previously into the light blue livery it carried when new. In 2012, 86233 was exported to Bulgaria as a source of spares for other Class 86s being used on freight services. 1 September 2002

The same programme of engineering work that led to West Coast services terminating at Milton Keynes also saw some freight trains being diverted over the Chiltern line on Saturdays. 66123 works the 11.46 Daventry-Dollands Moor intermodal round the curve to the south of Princes Risborough station. Apart from these diversions, in 2001 the only booked freights on this line all diverged from the main line at Princes Risborough station, taking the route to Aylesbury and onwards to the waste disposal site at Calvert. The old sidings on the left have since been refurbished for use by the heritage Chinnor and Princes Risborough Railway. 21 September 2002

Running on the third rail electrified system, Eurostar 3101/3102 working the 11.53 Waterloo International-Paris Gare du Nord have been diverted via Maidstone East due to weekend engineering work and are just curving off that line to join their normal route at Ashford. The new HS1 route under construction on the right would open with the initial stretch from Dollands Moor to Fawkham Junction eleven months later on 28 September 2003. 19 October 2002. (Antony Guppy)

The West Coast Main Line was closed for engineering work during the whole of the Easter Weekend 2003 and Royal Mail trains on Good Friday were diverted via the Chilterns. 67012 leads the 15.00 Warrington-Willesden mail towards Princes Risborough station. In 2011, a through line was added here as part of Chiltern's Evergreen Three project so a fast train could overtake one stopped in the up platform. The leading coach is a PCV (Propelling Control Vehicle) which was converted from a Class 307 unit driving trailer and intended to provide a cab for use when the train was being reversed in depots at low speed. 18 April 2003

In 2003, as in 2002, diversions of Wolverhampton-Euston services via Nuneaton took place for the whole of the summer timetable, from 18 May to 27 September. 57302 passes Washwood Heath Yard in charge of the 09.19 Wolverhampton-Euston with 86229 on the rear. The sidings on the left serve the unloading point for aggregates. The distinctive gas holders in the background which feature in many photographs were built in 1923 and, like many others throughout the country, became disused as a result of the newer method of storing gas underground. They were demolished in 2015. 13 July 2003

Although Class 57/3s were being used on diverted West Coast trains in 2003, Class 47s still appeared. Previously used by Great Western and still carrying the remains of their green livery, 47830 rounds the curve near the site of Nuneaton Abbey Junction with 86247 and the 12.35 Euston-Wolverhampton. The line in the picture has overhead electrification but in place it is never used as the wiring ends just behind the photographer. 13 July 2003

From May 2003 to September 2004, a temporary hourly service was introduced between St Pancras and Manchester due to engineering work on the West Coast main line affecting the Euston-Manchester service. Known as Project Rio and operated by Midland Mainline it mainly featured HST sets formerly used by Virgin Cross Country, plus a set from First Great Western. In this picture, the 15.00 St Pancras-Manchester Piccadilly departs from its Wellingborough stop with former FGW power car 43009 leading a mixed set of coaches and former Virgin power car 43088 on the rear. 29 August 2003

In August 2003, the West Coast Main Line was closed for a two week blockade while engineering work was carried out in the Ledburn Junction/Bourne End area. Mail trains were diverted via the Midland Main Line to get to and from the Willesden mail terminal. With 47773 providing power and towing 90035, the 15.32 Warrington-Willesden RMT passes through Wellingborough. The large brick building on the right is the old engine shed which ceased railway use in 1966. Although an attractive historic building, it was not deemed worthy of national listing by English Heritage. 29 August 2003

In the Bristol area in June 2004 the line between Narroways Hill Junction and Filton was closed for two weeks for the building of a third platform and associated trackwork at Filton Abbey Wood station. Wessex Trains to Cardiff and Virgin Cross Country trains to Gloucester were diverted via Avonmouth. This required careful pathing as the line from Narroways Hill Junction to Avonmouth is mostly single track. From Hallen Marsh to Filton the normally freight only line had been redoubled in 1994 for coal traffic. With the River Severn in the background, a Virgin Voyager unit leaves Hallen Marsh with the 12.25 Plymouth-Newcastle. 21 June 2004. (Stewart Jolly)

At Hallen Marsh Junction, 158749 and 158866 forming the 11.40 Cardiff Central-Portsmouth Harbour, operated by Wessex Trains, join the line from Severn Beach. These trains, along with Virgin Cross Country, ran hourly in each direction. To provide line capacity, the local trains calling at all stations to Severn Beach were cancelled and replaced by buses. Coal trains from Avonmouth to Didcot were suspended during the two week period. Just visible in the right background is shunter 09003 outside the Massy Wilcox freight terminal. 25 June 2004. (Stewart Jolly)

In summer 2004, Ipswich tunnel was closed for two months so that enlargement work could take place to accommodate freight trains carrying 9ft 6in containers. The daily container train from Felixstowe to Tilbury was diverted via Bury St Edmunds, Cambridge, Audley End and Tottenham Hale, using the line from Chippenham Junction to Cambridge that does not normally carry freight trains. 57008 is seen working this train through Newmarket. The locomotive was rebuilt by Brush from 47060 in 2000 and worked for Freightliner for just seven years before being withdrawn and leased to DRS. 29 July 2004

Four through passenger trains between Norwich and Liverpool Street, two each way, were diverted every weekday via Cambridge with Class 47 haulage throughout but with the electric locomotive still attached to the coach set. Here we see 86215 at Lakenheath on the rear of the first Norwich-bound train of the day, the 11.47 Liverpool Street-Norwich. 47813 was on the front. The station here is over three miles from the village of the same name and is one of the least used in the country. From 2015 to 2019 there were less than 500 passengers using the station per year on average – fewer than two per day. 1 September 2004

Anglia-liveried 47714 passes the delightful signal box and co-acting semaphore signals at Thetford with the 11.47 Liverpool Street-Norwich. 90012 is on the rear. Dating from 1883, the signal box closed in 2012 when the line was re-signalled. The railway was opened from Brandon to Trowse (just outside Norwich) through Thetford in 1845. On the left is the goods loading platform and, just beyond the platform a remarkable survivor – a loading gauge – which was used to ensure loaded freight wagons could fit within the railway without hitting infrastructure or other trains. 6 August 2004

One-liveried 47818 passes Shepreth Branch Junction with the 17.27 Liverpool Street-Norwich. 90003 is on the rear. 'One' was the branding for trains run by National Express East Anglia who took over the Greater Anglia Franchise in April 2004. 47818 was owned by Cotswold Rail and hired to National Express, having been repainted into One livery in July 2004, just a month before the photo was taken. 6 August 2004

In February and March 2005, diversions of West Coast Main Line services through Manchester took place every Saturday and Sunday. The diverted services ran between Euston, Preston and Liverpool Lime Street and used the route through Manchester Piccadilly, Oxford Road and Ordsall Lane Junction. On Easter Sunday, 57301 approaches Manchester Oxford Road with a Class 390 unit forming the 10.58 Longsight-Preston empty stock. This location twenty years earlier features on page 19. Following construction of the Windsor link (1988) and Ordsall Curve (2017) this became one of the busiest stretches of double track passenger railway in the country. 27 March 2005

57301 + 390002 pass through Bolton station with the 13.58 Preston-Euston. The recess for the Dellner coupling in the front of the locomotive is clearly visible and contrasts with the earlier smooth appearance of these locomotives in 2003 on page 72. The line here has since been electrified. Originally intended for completion in late 2017, it was finally ready for electric train services in 2019 after overcoming a series of engineering setbacks. 27 March 2005

The routing of trains to Liverpool Lime Street involved running through Manchester Piccadilly and Oxford Road stations, then taking the Chat Moss route via Castlefield Junction and Ordsall Lane Junction. 390012 is seen at Astley on the rear of the 12.33 Euston-Liverpool Lime Street with 57310 out of sight on the front. The signal box, of BR standard design and dating from 1972, supervises a small level crossing. It was retained to control the crossing when the line through here was electrified in 2015. 27 March 2005

On the weekend of 2/3 April 2005, the South West main line through Surbiton was closed for engineering work and a limited through service was run via Chertsey, Staines and Hounslow to Waterloo. This included Class 442 units operating services between Waterloo and Poole which were rarely seen away from the main line. The location is near Egham with the towers of Royal Holloway college just visible behind the train. The Class 442 units were withdrawn in 2007, refurbished and put on Gatwick services, withdrawn again in 2017 and a small number put back in service with South Western Railway in 2019. The coronavirus pandemic intervened in 2020 and they were stored again, then sent for scrap. 2 April 2005

On the same day 159009 + 008 pass through Chertsey station with a diverted Waterloo-Exeter service. The diverted route via Clapham Junction, Barnes, Hounslow, Staines, Virginia Water, Chertsey, and Woking is much longer and slower than the direct route through Wimbledon. The original station at Chertsey was the terminus of a line from Weybridge. The ornate station building, now Grade II listed, was built in 1866 when the line was extended to Virginia Water. 2 April 2005

In 2005 a new Tesco supermarket was being built at Gerrards Cross on a site spanning the railway when the roof of this new tunnel partly collapsed on 30 June. All train services were halted for two months while it was rebuilt. Bin liner trains to Calvert were diverted via Oxford and Islip with the loco running round at Claydon Junction to reach Calvert from the north. 66561 working the Dagenham-Calvert bin liner passes Cholsey on the Great Western Main Line. 19 July 2005

Freightliner's 57006 passes through Slough with a Wentloog-Southampton liner. It was booked to run Didcot-Reading West-Basingstoke-Winchester to Southampton but was diverted on a much longer route via West London: Didcot-Reading-Slough-Acton Wells Junction-Kensington Olympia-Clapham Junction-Barnes-Hounslow-Chertsey-Woking-Basingstoke-Winchester. This was due to signalling problems between Basingstoke and Reading. 15 March 2006

In March and April 2006 there were West Coast Main Line diversions over the Settle & Carlisle on some weekends involving Virgin Voyagers and Class 57/3 locomotives towing Pendolino units. 57307 tows 390032 on the 07.35 Glasgow Central-Euston near the site of the water troughs at Ling Gill, south of Garsdale. Beginning in 2010, Virgin released all their locomotives back to the leasing company Porterbrook. 57307 was leased to DRS in 2013 who hired it to Virgin West Coast and their successor Avanti West Coast for use as a standby locomotive in case of Pendolino failure. 4 March 2006. (John Turner)

57306 towing 390043 works the 13.49 Glasgow Central-Euston past Blea Moor signal box. The train has just entered the single track section which runs to Ribblehead Station and was created to prevent the additional loading on Ribblehead Viaduct caused by the weight of two trains passing After being released back to Porterbrook, 57306 was leased by DRS and then taken on long term hire by Great Western Railway for use on empty sleeper train workings between Paddington and Reading Depot. It occasionally works sleeper trains to Penzance when substituting for a failed GWR locomotive. 4 March 2006. (John Turner)

Diversions via Nuneaton were much less common once the upgrades on the main West Coast route had been completed in the early 2000s. Nevertheless, on the weekend of 15/16 July 2006 diverted services were operated with Class 390 Pendolino units hauled by Class 57s. Whitacre Junction is the location for this view from a public foot crossing of 57305 hauling 390022 on the 11.20 Euston-Wolverhampton. 15 July 2006

At Whitacre Junction on the same day, 57313 hauls 390010 on the 10.18 Wolverhampton-Euston. In this view, the Dellner coupler for connecting to Class 390 Pendolino units can be clearly seen in the large recess on the front of the locomotive. The line on the right is a headshunt for Hams Hall container depot which is just out of sight around the curve behind the train. 15 July 2006

There had been no passenger train diversions via Spalding since the aborted programme in 1991 but in January 2007 there were several diverted freights on Saturdays. In this view at Spalding, 66501 heads north with a Felixstowe-Leeds liner. This location appears several times in this book as it is one of my favourites. Since the picture on page 30 was taken in 1991 another siding has been removed and a lot of vegetation has grown up. Compare also with the 2018 shot on page 109. 20 January 2007

The Leeds-Ipswich liner operated by GB Railfreight (Gbrf) featured four Class 66 locomotives. Only the front one was working, and the others were included for positioning purposes to save track access charges from Network Rail. 66714 + 66721 + 66718 + 66537 approach the sweeping curve north of Donington village. Just visible in the bank beside the track are stumps where the old telegraph poles have been cut off. 20 January 2007

For two weeks in April 2007 trains were unable to take their usual route to Southampton Docks through Winchester due to an engineering blockade at Basingstoke and were instead diverted via Westbury, Salisbury and Romsey. 66510 is seen at Little Langford in the scenic Wylye Valley with a Garston-Southampton liner. This train had been routed from the north via Oxford, Didcot, Chippenham and Melksham to Westbury. 14 April 2007

Freightliner's 66567 passes through Warminster station with a Southampton-Ditton liner. On this day there were more than twenty diverted Freightliner and EWS liner trains to and from the container depots at Millbrook and Southampton Docks, with the majority being Freightliner-worked. The main freight traffic here on a normal day is stone from the quarries at Merehead and Whatley and a handful of engineers' trains between Westbury and Eastleigh. The attractive wooden station buildings date from 1851 when the line from Westbury was opened by the Great Western Railway with Warminster being the terminus. 11 April 2007

On 3 November 2007, engineering work on the West Coast main line saw a handful of intermodal trains diverted via the Chiltern line. 66044 is seen near Saunderton with a Hams Hall-Dollands Moor intermodal. Between this point and Princes Risborough, the two running lines diverge. The down line (on the left) mostly follows the route of the original Great Western single track branch line from Maidenhead to Aylesbury with a sweeping curve into Princes Risborough to avoid a steep gradient and the need for a tunnel. The up line was constructed in 1905 when the line to Aynho Junction was built. Leaving Princes Risborough southwards, it passes round a sharp curve and through a short tunnel to reach the location in the picture. 3 November 2007

Around New Year 2007/8 a number of mail trains were diverted via Oxford as the West Coast Main Line was blocked by various engineering works which included track remodelling at Rugby. 47847 hauls 325011 + 008 through Reading with a Wembley-Warrington mail train. The Class 325 units normally work on 25kV overhead electrification technology, so they had to be towed over these non-electrified lines. Digital camera technology has allowed a moving train at night to be captured without speed blur. 2 January 2008

In August 2008, when the West Coast main line was closed for several weekends, an alternative Euston-Birmingham service was operated by Virgin on the Chiltern route. One of the diagrams featured a Class 57/3 locomotive hauling a spare set of Mark 3 coaches which made one run in each direction. 57313 approaches Princes Risborough with the 11.00 Euston-Wolverhampton. The line to the left is the up line (to London) which takes a shorter alignment to Saunderton. 17 August 2008

The majority of the Virgin services to Birmingham used Class 221 Voyager units which can be distinguished from their Class 220 sisters by having five coaches. 221109 enters West Ruislip station with the 11.45 Birmingham International-Euston. To reach Euston involves taking several connecting spurs that do not normally see passenger trains and running via Northolt, South Greenford, Acton Main Line, Acton Wells Junction and West London Junction. The four car Class 220 Voyagers were all used on Cross Country services. 23 August 2008

The West Coast Main Line closure continued to the Tuesday following August Bank Holiday Monday which meant that the Gbrf-operated mail trains had to take an alternative route. 57303 has been hired to work with 325012 + 008 and is seen at Iver with the evening Wembley-Warrington working. A Class 57/3 was very rare on this route at the time. In later years, a Class 57/3 hired from DRS could often be seen on the empty stock workings for the Great Western Night Riviera sleeper service. 26 August 2008

The Wrexham, Shropshire and Marylebone Railway was a short lived open access operator that ran trains between Wrexham and Marylebone via Telford, Wolverhampton and the Chiltern route. Initially the trains were top and tailed by Class 67s, then when DVT coaches were ready a single Class 67 was used. Trains often passed through Birmingham New Street but were not permitted to pick up or set down passengers. When Marylebone was closed on Sunday, 21 September, they ran their afternoon train into Paddington via South Ruislip, Greenford and Park Royal. 67013 top and tailed with 67025 pass North Acton Central Line station while working the 10.02 Ruabon-Paddington. 21 September 2008

The North London Line through Canonbury and Highbury & Islington stations was closed for four months in summer 2009 to allow rebuilding work to take place. Freight trains to and from the Great Eastern Main Line were diverted over the Gospel Oak-Barking line with Class 66 diesel power towing the electric locomotive and its train. 66541 and 90041 with Felixstowe-Crewe liner pass Gospel Oak station. The platform here is used by trains to Barking, which at the time were Class 150 diesel units operated by London Overground. 29 May 2009

On the same day, 66541 hauls 90043 on a Ditton-Felixstowe liner past Harringay Park Junction signal box and its semaphore signals. The signal box, dating from 1959, closed in November 2009 when the line was re-signalled. The line in the right foreground leads to Harringay station on the King's Cross main line and carries freight trains only. Behind the train is Crouch Hill tunnel with a viaduct above it carrying the former line from Finsbury Park to Alexandra Palace which closed to passengers in 1954 and has been converted into the Parkland Walk. 29 May 2009

In summer 2009, the line between Doncaster and Scunthorpe was closed for ten weeks for embankment work to take place. Freight trains that would normally take this route were instead routed via Brigg or Market Rasen to Barnetby. 66547 with a Bredbury-Roxby bin liner passes Sykes Lane level crossing near Saxilby. The train will run through Lincoln to Barnetby before running round to reach Scunthorpe then running round again to get to the tip at Roxby. The signalling at Saxilby was modernised in 2014 with control passing to Lincoln signalling centre. 25 August 2009

66561 passes the unusually tall signal box at Kirton Lime Sidings with a West Burton power station to Immingham empty coal train. The line was singled from here to a point just east of Gainsborough Central station in the early 1980s. The sidings have been disused for many years and in 2009 were no longer connected to the main line. Built in 1886, the signal box is Grade II listed and was sympathetically refurbished by Network Rail in 2011. 27 August 2009

60004 with a Preston Docks-Lindsey empty tanks working has been diverted via the Brigg route and is seen at Gainsborough Central. It will regain its normal route at Barnetby. At the time the Brigg route normally saw no trains during the day and passenger trains only on Saturdays. After much campaigning by the Friends of the Brigg and Lincoln Line a weekday passenger service was introduced in 2019. 26 August 2009

On the weekend of 30/31 January, there was engineering work on the line between Leamington Spa and Banbury so Wrexham & Shropshire trains were diverted via the West Coast Main Line. 67010 passes Headstone Lane with the 07.23 Wrexham -Marylebone. The route to Marylebone was from here to Willesden, Acton Canal Wharf Jn, Acton Main Line, South Greenford, then to South Ruislip where it reversed and picked up its normal route. 30 January 2010

On 5 September 2010, Wrexham & Shropshire trains were due to be diverted via the West Coast Main line instead of taking their usual route to Marylebone on the Chiltern main line. Due to signalling problems in the Wolverton area, it was decided instead to send the 11.20 Wrexham-Marylebone via Banbury, Oxford and Reading. Unfortunately, due to a lack of route knowledge by the guard, the train had to run empty from Banbury. 67013 passes through Taplow with the Banbury-Marylebone empty stock working. 5 September 2010

In October 2010 there were several weekends when East Coast Main Line trains were diverted over the GN & GE Joint line through Spalding and Lincoln. Here is a busy scene at Sleaford North as 67019 rounds the curve on the line from Sleaford West with the 11.00 King's Cross-Leeds while in the background an HST set heads south on the Sleaford Avoiding Line with the 10.33 Newcastle-King's Cross. The disused northbound track of the Sleaford Avoiding Line can be clearly seen here with rusty rails and grass growing on the track bed. 9 October 2010

The Saturday diversions began around lunchtime. In this view at Sleaford North, two workings are passing: on the left East Coast 43058 + 082 with the 11.30 King's Cross-Newcastle and on the right Hull Trains 180110 waits at the signal with the 11.19 Hull-King's Cross for the line to clear. The HST set had been hired from East Midlands Trains. The line was re-signalled in 2014 and all the semaphore signals removed. 9 October 2010

Wrexham & Shropshire services were diverted via the West Coast main line again on the weekend of 9/10 October 2010 but took a different route in West London compared with previous occasions. From Wrexham trains ran via Bletchley to Willesden, then Willesden Junction (Acton Branch) to Acton Canal Wharf Junction where the train reversed and headed north. It then branched left at Neasden Junction to reach the Chiltern line where it reversed again to head toward Marylebone. In this view, 67013 rounds the curve at Neasden Junction with the 10.55 Wrexham-Marylebone. This curve had not been used by a scheduled passenger train for many years. 10 October 2010

With Spalding skyline in the background, 67029 hauls 91111 on the 14.00 King's Cross-Leeds towards Gosberton. 67029 was painted into this silver livery in 2004 to match the EWS Company Train which it normally hauled. On this day, all the Leeds trains were formed of Class 91 sets hauled by a Class 67 while most of the remaining East Coast trains were HSTs. The Class 91 is normally at the north end of the set, as on this train. 16 October 2010

Autumn colours are in abundance as 67019 hauls 91117 on the 13.05 Leeds-King's Cross through Gosberton. Unusually the coaching set is in reverse formation with the Class 91 at the south end. The crossing keeper has worked quickly and already closed the gates behind the train. There has been a great deal of change and vegetation growth at this location since the 1982 picture on Page 14. 16 October 2010

Over Christmas 2010 and the New Year period the Great Western Main Line through Reading was closed for remodelling and re-signalling work. Trains from London to the West Country ran out of Waterloo while trains to Bristol and South Wales were diverted via Banbury to reach Paddington. The much-extended journey to Paddington involved leaving the main line at Didcot, running to Banbury where trains reversed and then taking the Chiltern Line at Aynho Junction as far as South Ruislip. From there they took the mainly single track line through Greenford to regain the main line at Old Oak Common. First Great Western's 43156 + 071 on the 08.23 Swansea-Paddington approaches Gerrards Cross station while Chiltern's 165007 passes on the 12.24 Marylebone-Bicester North. 29 December 2010

HST 43193 runs along the single track line from Old Oak Common to Park Royal with the 12.45 Paddington-Bristol Temple Meads and is seen beside the Central Line tracks at North Acton. This was once the Great Western Railway's main line from Paddington to Birkenhead. In the 2010/11 timetable the line saw just one scheduled passenger train each weekday – the 11.36 from Paddington to High Wycombe operated by Chiltern Railways – with no inbound service. 1 January 2011

For a four month period in spring and summer 2011, engineering work on Arnside Viaduct meant that through trains could not run. Flask trains between power stations in southern Britain and Sellafield had to be diverted along the northern route into Sellafield via the West Coast Main Line, Maryport and Workington. 57003 + 007 are seen at Beckfoot on the West Coast main line heading for Carlisle while working the 06.30 Crewe-Sellafield with a flask that originated at Bridgwater. Flask trains never normally run on this stretch of line. The train will leave the main line at Upperby Bridge Junction and join the Cumbrian Coast route at Currock Junction. 28 June 2011

Flask workings normally use a pair of locomotives in double headed formation to provide resilience against one of the locomotives failing. In this picture of a Sellafield-Heysham flask working at Harrington the pair of locomotives (57007 and 003) is in top and tailed formation to simplify reversal at Morecambe station on the last leg of the run to Heysham power station. The path behind the train is the track bed of a siding that used to serve Workington steel works. 19 May 2011

On the Sunday of the 2012 May Day Bank Holiday weekend, the West Coast Main Line was closed for engineering work and Virgin Trains ran a special service via the Chiltern route. Most of the trains were formed of Class 221 Voyager units but one diagram featured 57315 and 57308 top and tailing a set of Mark 3 coaches that Virgin used for a small number of weekday timetabled services. 57315 in Arriva livery leads the 11.11 Euston-Nuneaton past Northolt station on the Central Line. The train has had to take a tour of West London connecting lines to get to this point: Euston-West London Junction-Acton Wells Junction-Acton Main Line-West Ealing Junction-Greenford. 6 May 2012

In 2012 the oil depot at Colnbrook was mainly supplied by Lindsey oil refinery on Humberside. Trains normally ran down the Midland Main Line and across West London to reach West Drayton and the Colnbrook branch. An extra working occasionally ran via Didcot on Saturdays where it was stabled overnight before setting off for Colnbrook on Sunday morning. This routing involved a reversal at Southall Yard. 60059 hauls the Lindsey/Didcot-Colnbrook oil away from Twyford. 22 July 2012

The Easter 2013 closure of the Great Western Main Line for rebuilding work at Reading saw services between South Wales and Paddington diverted via Didcot, Banbury (reverse), Princes Risborough and Park Royal. 43162 + 142 on the 05.27 Swansea-Paddington pass the distinctive Great Western pagoda-style corrugated iron waiting shelters at Denham Golf Club. This station was opened in 1912, seven years after the line opened in 1905, as part of a plan to encourage more local usage. 29 March 2013

While the Great Western main line at Reading was closed, West of England services ran into Waterloo via Westbury, Salisbury and the South Western main line. On the evening of Easter Monday 43161 + 126 pass through Weybridge on the down fast line with the 17.07 Waterloo-Penzance. First Great Western ran an hourly service of HSTs in each direction, travelling via Basingstoke and Salisbury before picking up their normal route at Westbury. 1 April 2013

On the weekend of 1/2 June 2013, services on the East Coast main line were diverted via Lincoln, Sleaford and Spalding to Peterborough. The Sleaford Avoiding line had been closed since the 1980s in the northbound direction due to track damage caused by a derailment while the southbound line remained open. East Coast 43310 + 313 with the 12.30 King's Cross-Aberdeen have turned off the GN&GE Joint Line at Sleaford South Junction and are about to join the Skegness line (on the left) to pass through Sleaford station. They will then turn north at Sleaford West Junction before re-joining the Joint line at Sleaford North Junction as shown on page 92. 1 June 2013

Hull Trains 180111 is seen approaching a public foot crossing on the Sleaford Avoiding Line with the 14.52 Hull-King's Cross. During this period the avoiding line was being rebuilt so that the disused northbound track could be brought back into service for freight trains in 2014 when the line was re-signalled. Note the new concrete troughing on the left for cables, the freshly laid ballast and rusty rails. 1 June 2013

During rebuilding of the Oxford-Bicester line, freight trains to the MoD depot at Bicester were unable to take their normal route Didcot-Oxford-Bicester. Instead, they had to take a long diversion and run Didcot-Reading-South Greenford-South Ruislip-Princes Risborough-Aylesbury to the run round loop at Claydon LNE Junction. This view shows 67005 with a couple of vans forming the 07.32 Didcot-Bicester approaching the public foot crossing at Charndon just after running round. It is on the final leg of its journey on the single track line between Claydon LNE Junction and Bicester. This line is being rebuilt and upgraded to a double track line with passenger services as part of the East-West Railway project. 3 July 2014

The diversion of MoD trains to Bicester via Aylesbury continued for a couple of years until the Bicester-Oxford line upgrade was completed throughout at the end of 2016. 66118 with a single van nears Princes Risborough working the 07.32 Didcot-Bicester on the part of the route where the up and down tracks are separated. The line used by the train here is the course of the original GWR single track branch line from Maidenhead to Aylesbury. 19 January 2016

The West Coast main line was closed on a number of weekends in the 2010s which prevented through running of the overnight Anglo-Scottish sleeper trains. When this happened in early 2016, the up sleepers ran into King's Cross instead of Euston. The stock then had to get to Wembley for servicing. On the morning of Saturday 30 January, 87002 is seen approaching Harringay station with the empty sleeper stock with 90043 out of sight on the rear. It will run as far as Ferme Park Carriage Sidings where the train will reverse and 90043 will take over. The train will then head south over Harringay flyover before taking the King's Cross Incline to join the North London line and reach Wembley via Primrose Hill. 30 January 2016

On several weekends in February 2016, the line to Fort William was blocked by engineering work north of Crianlarich so the Caledonian sleeper was diverted to Oban. Route availability prevented Class 67s working to Oban so the newly rebuilt Class 73/9 locomotives made their debut on these sleeper trains. Due to a lack of facilities at Oban, the stock was taken to Polmadie for servicing. 73967 crosses Loch Awe with the 10.30 Oban-Polmadie empty stock working. 27 February 2016. (John Turner)

In August 2016 there was a week-long blockade at Banbury to implement track and signalling changes. Freight trains to and from Southampton were diverted via the West Coast and Great Western main lines. 66121 passes through Taplow station with Ford cars and vans from Southampton to Garston. Although the delightful Great Western wooden footbridge was listed it was damaged during an engineering possession and closed to passengers as can be seen here. It was eventually replaced by a new structure with lifts at the other end of the station and demolished. 8 August 2016

The Oxford-Bicester line was re-opened in stages. Initially the stretch from Oxford Parkway to Bicester opened in October 2015 with passenger trains running via the new Gavray Junction to Marylebone. The stretch between Oxford Parkway and Oxford remained out of use until December 2016. This meant that stone trains to the Banbury Road terminal beside Oxford Parkway station had to run via Bicester. The method of operation was to run the wagons as a portion of a jumbo train to Acton Yard, then haul them via West Ruislip, Princes Risborough and Gavray Junction. In this view at Oddington, 59103 hauls empty stone wagons from Banbury Road to Acton Yard. 29 November 2016

The Welsh main line between Bridgend and Margam was closed for engineering work on Sunday, 8 January 2017. Passenger trains were replaced by buses, but freight continued to run by diverting trains via Tondu which required a run round and reversal at Tondu Middle Junction. 60091 approaches Tondu on the line from Bridgend with a Margam-Llanwern steel train. This line is freight only and, with the demise of the local coal industry, sees no regular traffic. 8 January 2017. (Paul Davis)

On the weekend of 5/6 February 2017, the East Coast main line was closed between Hitchin and Peterborough with all through trains diverted via Cambridge and March. A few locations on this route still feature semaphore signalling, including Whittlesea which also has manually operated crossing gates. Note how the tall gate support posts are made of concrete which is a characteristic of former LNER lines. HST 43308 + 208 approach a foggy Whittlesea with the 07.55 Newcastle-King's Cross. Strangely, the spelling of the station name is different to the village (Whittlesey). 5 February 2017

Hull Trains services were also diverted. At the time they were all operated by Alstom-built Class 180 diesel units. 180113 passes March South signal box working the 12.30 Hull-King's Cross. Worthy of note is the British Railways era dark blue enamel sign on the signal box dating from the 1950s. When originally built in 1876, the signal box was called Nene Junction and was renamed in 1928. 5 February 2017

Grand Central have been operating services from King's Cross to Sunderland since 2007 and to Bradford since 2009. One of their buffer-fitted HST sets with power cars 43484 + 465 approaches Manea station with the 09.20 Sunderland-King's Cross. Semaphore signals located on the opposite side of the line were once commonplace but rare on Network Rail by 2017. Note the siding beside the train which can no longer be used as the point switch blades have been removed. 5 February 2017

On Saturday 5 February, just five of the Virgin East Coast services in daylight hours featured Class 91 sets hauled by Class 67 locomotives. The remainder were formed of HST sets. 67021 with 91101 on the 12.47 King's Cross-Leeds pass a snow plough in a siding at March. Although not easily seen from this angle, 91101 carries a special Flying Scotsman livery. Beside the train is a semaphore signal with a pair of miniature arms used for signalling movements in the down loop. Each arm corresponds to a different route that can be taken. 5 February 2017

On the weekend of 17/18 September the Great Western Main Line was closed at Reading for rebuilding work and trains to Paddington were diverted via Didcot, Oxford, the newly rebuilt line to Bicester, then via Princes Risborough, South Ruislip and Greenford. GWR's 0936 Bristol Temple Meads-Paddington with HST power cars 43128 + 180 passes Chiltern's 10.05 Marylebone-Oxford at Oxford Parkway. This station was built at the Oxford Park & Ride site near Kidlington and opened in 2015. 17 September 2017

Among the Great Western passenger trains a freight train was also diverted. 66198 leads the Acton-Severnside bin liner round the curve at Bicester Gavray Junction and will shortly join the only remaining operational section of the Bletchley-Oxford line. Above the train can be seen the Chiltern main line through Bicester North station. At the time this train ran every weekday and occasional Sundays. Yellow containers were used to serve the Northolt and Brentford refuse loading terminals. 17 September 2017

In September and October 2017, the East Coast Main Line north of Newcastle was closed for four weekends and Virgin East Coast trains to and from Edinburgh were diverted via Carlisle. Most of the diverted trains were operated by HSTs and there were just a couple of electric trains in each direction which needed to be hauled by Class 67 locomotives between Carlisle and Newcastle. The 06.50 Glasgow Central-King's Cross with 67008 hauling 91129 passes Gilsland. 30 September 2017. (Brian Carter)

On Sunday, 10 June 2018, Marylebone station was closed for track works and a limited service of two Chiltern Railways trains each way per hour was run into Paddington. These services used the line between South Ruislip and Old Oak Common through Greenford. 168106 passes Park Royal with the 14.59 Paddington-Birmingham Snow Hill. Behind the train is the track bed of the old siding which served the Guinness brewery and closed in 1995. In December 2018, the stretch of line from Greenford to Old Oak Common closed to allow HS2 construction work to commence. 10 June 2018

The East Coast Main Line was closed between Werrington Junction (Peterborough) and Doncaster for the whole weekend of 10/11 November 2018 with diversions via Doncaster-Lincoln-Sleaford Avoiding Line-Spalding-Peterborough. By this time the main operator of services on the East Coast main line was LNER and their HST power cars 43314 + 302 approach Spalding station with the 08.30 Edinburgh Waverley-King's Cross. The photographer is standing on the same station footbridge as for the HST picture on Page 13. Although the train is similar in both pictures the only other unchanged items in 36 years are the station canopy and the pillar on the right at the end of the platform. 10 November 2018

After a torrential downpour, 67012 and 91106 pass Golden High Hedges Level Crossing near Quadring (north of Spalding) working the 13.15 Leeds-King's Cross. Just five of the LNER workings on this day during daylight hours were Class 67s hauling Class 91 sets, all of them running between Leeds and King's Cross. 67012 is still in the silver and grey livery originally applied when it was a member of the dedicated pool of locomotives for Wrexham & Shropshire services which ceased operations in early 2011. 10 November 2018

67028 in bright red DB Cargo livery hauls the 09.03 King's Cross-Leeds with 91110 through Spalding. The locomotive has been repainted in the same shade of red used by DB locomotives in Germany. Five months previously, LNER took over the East Coast franchise from Virgin after they ran into financial difficulties. The livery of the Class 91 and coaching stock is standard Virgin East Coast livery updated with LNER branding. 10 November 2018

In late 2018, LNER hired a full HST set and two power cars from East Midlands Trains to provide additional capacity. The power cars (43075 and 43061) are seen here at Spalding with a set of LNER Mark 3 coaches working the 10.00 King's Cross-Edinburgh Waverley. The railway used to continue straight on to Boston and Grimsby until most of the East Lincolnshire lines were closed in 1970 leaving just the line to Skegness. One of the tracks was retained until 1980 as a siding to serve the sugar beet factory. 10 November 2018

The daily Westbury-Bescot engineering service is booked to run via Melksham and Swindon to Didcot where it takes the Oxford line to stop over in Hinksey Yard. On 17 January 2019 there were signalling problems at Swindon, so the train was diverted via Newbury and Reading West to Didcot. Colas Rail's 70806 with its train of loaded Network Rail ballast wagons crosses the Kennet & Avon canal on the approach to Hungerford. At the time there were no Colas-operated trains booked over this route. 17 January 2019

In early 2019, Whiteball Tunnel near Taunton was closed for three weeks for extensive engineering work. Trains between Paddington and the West Country were diverted via the London & South Western route through Yeovil and Honiton. Due to capacity constraints on the mostly single track route the GWR trains ran every two hours in each direction. GWR 43198 + 088 work the 09.03 Paddington-Plymouth through Yeovil Pen Mill on the line from Castle Cary to Weymouth. 26 February 2019

GWR 43160 + 192 pass through the station at Crewkerne with the 11.03 Paddington-Plymouth. The signal box at the end of the platform had a short working life, being opened in 1960 to replace an older structure but was closed in 1967 when the South Western line was singled. The single track section through here runs between Yeovil Junction and the passing loop at Chard Junction. 26 February 2019

With the Whiteball Tunnel diversions in operation, GWR 43063 + 004 work the 09.16 Plymouth-Paddington past Coker Wood, to the west of Yeovil Junction. The cutting sides here were heavily wooded until 2018 when they were cleared by Network Rail. Timekeeping of the diverted trains had to be good to avoid causing extensive delays when other trains have to wait at the passing loops between single line sections. 26 February 2019

For two weeks from 20 July to 4 August, engineering work for the new Barking Riverside branch at Ripple Lane saw westbound freight trains from London Gateway and Tilbury routed via the single track Grays-Upminster line. 66563 approaches Ockendon station with a London Gateway-Garston intermodal. Just westbound freights were diverted, and eastbound freights continued over their usual route. This line normally only sees passenger trains plus test trains and, in the leaf fall season, a railhead treatment train. 2 August 2019. (Antony Guppy)

During the weekend of 18/19 January 2020, the East Coast main line was closed between Hitchin and Peterborough with all trains being diverted via Cambridge and March. Hull Trains 802302 passes Addenbrookes, south of Cambridge, with the 10.40 Hull-King's Cross. At the time the unit was new and had only been in service for about a month. The futuristic looking buildings behind the train are part of the Cambridge Biomedical Campus which is the largest centre for medical science in Europe. 18 January 2020

During a full weekend of diversions, LNER's 800103 passes Cambridge station on the through line working the 06.55 Edinburgh Waverley-King's Cross. Throughout the day, LNER ran an hourly train in each direction with all services formed of Hitachi Class 800 series units running on diesel power despite the line being electrified. This is the same location as the picture on page 10 separated by 40 years. The changes are huge and only the station building in the distance remains the same. 18 January 2020

On 28 January 2020, a container train derailed in Eastleigh station causing damage to the track. Passenger trains between Southampton and Waterloo were unable to run through the station and a few through trains were diverted via Havant. Most freight trains to/from Southampton Docks are routed via Eastleigh so they were also unable to run to the north. Container trains from the Western Docks instead ran via Romsey, Salisbury Laverstock Curve and Andover to regain their normal route at Basingstoke. To avoid the need to run round, car trains to/from the Eastern docks ran via Havant, Guildford and Wokingham before regaining their normal route at Reading. In this picture the 10.07 Cowley-Southampton Eastern Docks headed by 66136 runs through Wokingham towards Guildford. The Reading-Guildford line has no regular booked freight workings. There has been relatively little change at this location in the nineteen years since the picture on page 65 was taken. 1 February 2020

In October/November 2020, the Great Western main line through the Severn Tunnel was closed due to rebuilding a bridge at Patchway. Passenger trains to/from London Paddington were diverted via Lydney, Gloucester and Kemble. On a sunny autumnal morning with mist in the distance, the 07.44 Swansea-Paddington formed of 800005 + 800023 passes Churcham on the outskirts of Gloucester. In the background can be seen the hills of the Forest of Dean. 4 November 2020

The Bristol Kingsland Road based Railhead Treatment Train (RHTT) was also affected as it had to treat lines on both sides of the River Severn. To travel between Bristol and South Wales it ran via Yate, Gloucester and Chepstow. As it passes Gatcombe while returning to Bristol, 66846 can be seen on the rear while 66850 is on the front. Although operation of this RHTT was contracted to DB Cargo it was sub-contracted to Colas, hence the use of Colas Class 66/8 locomotives. 4 November 2020

Freight trains were also diverted due to the Patchway bridge works. Several container services run each day to the terminal at Wentloog, east of Cardiff. One of the Freightliner services, destined for Southampton Western Dock, can be seen at Churcham behind 66507. The train is made up of standard and low platform wagons to accommodate both regular containers (8 feet 6 inches high) and high cube containers (9ft 6in high) within the loading gauge. 4 November 2020

On the weekend of 5/6 December 2020 there were engineering works in the Wimbledon area which partially blocked the South West main line. Unusually, only certain services were diverted, in this case trains from Weymouth and Portsmouth to Waterloo. Trains from Waterloo to Weymouth and Portsmouth and Salisbury/Exeter trains in both directions were unaffected. 444010 + 026 round the sharp curve at Staines with the 06.55 Weymouth-Waterloo. Class 444 units are rarely seen on this route. 5 December 2020